BEYOND BORSCHT

Old-World Recipes from Eastern Europe
Ukraine, Russia, Poland & More

Tatyana Nesteruk

Founder of Tatyana's Everyday Food
and Author of *The European Cake Cookbook*

PAGE STREET
PUBLISHING CO.

PAGE STREET
PUBLISHING CO.

First published in 2020 by

Page Street Publishing Co.

27 Congress Street, Suite 105

Salem, MA 01970

www.pagestreetpublishing.com

Distributed by Macmillan, sales in Canada by The Canadian Manda Group.

24 23 22   4 5

ISBN-13: 978-1-62414-960-3

ISBN-10: 1-62414-960-X

Library of Congress Control Number: 2019943010

Cover and book design by Rosie Stewart for Page Street Publishing Co.

Photography by Tatyana Nesteruk

Printed and bound in the United States of America

DEDICATION

This cookbook is dedicated to the most hardworking, loving and caring individual I know:
my amazing mother, Galina. Thank you for instilling in me a love for cooking and
for the amazing recipes.

To my grandmother, Yuliya—thank you for your love, kindness and compassion and for all those
incredible cabbage piroshki and cheese pancakes. You'll always live on in my memories.

And to my great-grandmothers, Olga and Galina.

TABLE OF CONTENTS

INTRODUCTION

Beyond Borscht is a collection of old-world, nostalgic Eastern European recipes from Ukraine, Russia and Poland that have persevered over many years, through many generations and in many countries around the world. Every single recipe in this book is special in its own way and comes with much history. This book is one of the first of its kind: a tribute to incredible Slavic cuisine. I am excited, humbled and honored to have the opportunity to share this amazing, rich and varied cuisine with the world.

This cookbook has a little bit of everything—dishes for every day and every occasion, from easy soups and refreshing salads to hearty braised meats and tasty hand pies. There are also plenty of pickled and stuffed veggies. And this cookbook wouldn't be complete without some of the delicious desserts enjoyed in Slavic culture! There's a sweet treat for everyone, from easy and delicious creations such as cookies and waffles to elaborate, special-occasion cakes like Torte Napoleon (page 161). In these pages, you'll find a true tasting menu representing the colorful and unique cuisine of Eastern Europe.

So, what is it that makes Eastern European cuisine so special? This cuisine is a melting pot of rich flavors influenced by its storied history. Eastern Europe is a vast area, encompassing many countries in several regions: Ukraine, Romania, Belarus, Moldova and parts of Russia and Poland; the Baltic states of Estonia, Lithuania and Latvia; and the Caucasus nations Azerbaijan, Armenia and Georgia. In this cookbook, you'll find recipes primarily from Ukraine, Russia and Poland, where my family is originally from. Because Eastern Europe encompasses such a large area, you'll find many different types of cooking methods, ingredients and techniques. Cooking techniques can vary vastly between regions and seasons. During the summer months, open-fire and coal grilling is used for recipes like Shish Kebabs (page 60) and Beef and Garlic Rice Pilaf (page 53). During long winter months, food is either slow-braised, baked or deep-fried. Back in Ukraine, my grandparents used a печь (pech), a special type of wood-burning fireplace that could also be used for cooking. That type of fireplace is still used today in some villages, although modern stoves have taken over for the most part. You'll also find that most meat recipes are slow-braised, going back to the times when expensive cuts of meat were rare and not accessible to the general population. There's nothing like the aroma of a hearty, braised dish filling your home!

The cuisine of Eastern Europe is primarily based on ingredients that are readily available and store well. For example, root vegetables (such as beets, potatoes and carrots) are used in many savory recipes because they're so plentiful and easy to store during long winters. Heartier fruits (such as apples) also store well for longer periods of time and are used in many desserts. Almost every home in Ukraine and Russia has a root cellar for storing vegetables and canned goods or sauerkraut. Summer vegetables—such as cucumbers, tomatoes, zucchini and cabbage—are pickled or canned to help them last longer. Mushrooms are also a huge part of Eastern Europe's culinary tradition. Wild mushrooms are plentiful in Eastern Europe and can be pickled or dried. My parents often talk about how delicious the wild mushrooms were back in Ukraine. Seafood also accounts for a large part of Slavic cuisine. There are many lakes and rivers in the region, making fish and other seafood available almost year-round. The herbs and spices used are strong and fragrant, giving food incredible aroma and flavor. Common ones include dill, parsley, black pepper, cumin, paprika and coriander. Dill is used in just about everything, from sandwiches and appetizers to soups and pickled vegetables. It's the quintessential Eastern European herb, and you'll see it often in this cookbook. And let's not forget the cheese and dairy! *Tvorog* (quark), *smetana* (sour cream) and milk are also essential for many recipes.

In old-world Eastern Europe, cooking was primarily a women's affair with the exception of grilling outdoors, which was usually done by men. My grandmother would stay home with the kids and cook most of the day, preparing multiple dishes. A traditional Slavic dinner includes some sort of appetizer and cured meat like *salo* (salt-cured pork fat) or sausage, a salad, some pickled vegetables as a side and a hearty main dish, followed by tea and cake, cookies or a fruit dessert. It can take all day to prepare a meal like that! Nowadays, with new technology and a more modern way of life, cooking is taking up less time but remains just as important to the Slavic culture. If you ever get invited to a Ukrainian dinner, be prepared for a feast!

Because this cookbook has such a large variety of recipes, coming up with the title *Beyond Borscht* was not an easy task. *How do I correctly represent what's on the inside?* That was my dilemma. This collection of recipes represents my Eastern European heritage and the food I grew up with. However, as a Slavic transplant now living in the United States, I know that most people outside the Slavic cultural community may have never heard of or tasted anything but borscht. Borscht is one of the most iconic dishes of Eastern Europe's cuisine and almost everyone has tried some version of it. If only they knew what else Eastern Europe had to offer. And that's how the title was born—I wanted to give a nod to all the incredible recipes *beyond* borscht.

Writing this cookbook has been a trip down memory lane for me—every recipe has a story, a memory, an aroma that takes me back to my childhood. My passion for food started many years ago, when I was still a child. I have always loved food. I was born in Yekaterinburg, Russia, to Polish, Ukrainian and Romanian parents and raised in the United States from a young age. All I knew about food as I was growing up was Eastern European cuisine. Even at a very young age, I was excited to be in the kitchen, especially when my mom would let me help her shape pelmeni and piroshki. From the very start of my career in the food industry, I had a passion for sharing the delicious Eastern European dishes I grew

up with. As social media took off, I was encouraged by my family and friends to start sharing recipes on those platforms and on a personal website. I did just that, starting with classic recipes like beef borscht and cabbage piroshki on my YouTube channel, Tatyana's Everyday Food. Fast-forward several years: I had the opportunity to start my own food blog and become a cookbook author, and now I have the chance to share all the incredible old-world recipes that I learned from my mother and grandmother.

The recipes in this book are very important to Slavic culture. It's been a lifelong dream of mine to author this cookbook. In fact, I love these recipes so much that even before I had a blog, I wrote my very own Eastern European "cookbook," complete with photographs! In the Slavic community, it's a popular tradition for young women getting ready to move out of the family home to compile a handwritten collection of recipes passed down from their moms, aunts or grandmas. It's a tradition that's been passed down through generations—I remember my mom's old handwritten notebook, with its brown cover and blue grid pages. In some ways, *Beyond Borscht* is the upgraded, sophisticated version of that.

Eastern Europe has such rich history, culture and food that is still hidden away, like a gem aching to be discovered. The food is hearty, warming and made with love, to be savored with family and friends. If you're a Slavic person reading this book, I hope you enjoy these familiar recipes as much as you always have and that they reignite your love for traditional Eastern European food. If you're just discovering this incredible cuisine, I hope you dive right in and try the dish that seems most unique—perhaps even strange—to you. I guarantee it will be unlike anything you've tried. You're going to love it!

As we say in Russian: приятного аппетита (priyatnogo appetita; enjoy your meal)!

Tatyana

INGREDIENTS AND TOOLS

It's understandable that ingredients and tools vary between countries and regions and that some items used in this book might be difficult to source. I've put together some information on important and traditional items that will help you along the way.

TVOROG – ТВОРОГ: Also known as farmer cheese or quark, this soft, plain cheese is used in both savory and sweet recipes. This type of cheese is readily available in Russian or Eastern European markets but may be hard to find otherwise. Instead of using tvorog, I have substituted it with large-curd cottage cheese throughout this book. When cottage cheese is rinsed and just the curds remain, it becomes the perfect substitute for tvorog, and it's much easier to source! If you have tvorog, use that in place of the cottage cheese called for throughout the book.

SOUR CREAM – СМЕТАНА (SMET-ANA): Sour cream is called smetana in Eastern Europe and it's slightly different from the sour cream that is available in the United States. In Ukraine and Russia, sour cream isn't quite as thick, is less tart and is milder in flavor. It's used as a spread for bread, is added to soups and salads for creaminess and it's even used for dessert. Not to worry—the sour cream available in the United States will work just fine for all the recipes in this cookbook.

DILL – УКРОП (UKROP): Dill is the quintessential herb of Eastern European cuisine. This aromatic herb is used for seasoning soups, salads, main dishes and appetizers. A little bit of this refreshing herb goes a long way. In addition to being used in recipes, it's typically sprinkled over dishes as a garnish before serving. There isn't a substitute for dill, and I highly recommend adding it to recipes even if you don't typically enjoy it. It's an important part of the flavor profile of Eastern European cuisine.

HERRING – СЕЛЕДКА (SELODKA): Unlike the pickled herring in wine sauce that can be found in most US supermarkets, herring in Eastern Europe is marinated almost exclusively in oil, sometimes with onion and dill. Make sure to use this type of herring when it's called for in a recipe. Herring is typically served with bread and topped with sliced raw onion and dill and enjoyed as an appetizer.

SORREL – ЩАВЕЛЬ (SHCHAVEL'): Sorrel is a sour and slightly spicy herb that's used in my Sorrel and Chicken Green Borscht (page 78). In other cuisines, it's typically used sparingly but for my soup recipe, you'll need a large bundle. You can find large bundles of sorrel in most Eastern European markets during the summer months. Some stores do carry this herb next to more common ones like basil and dill but in much smaller quantities. If you enjoy sorrel, I recommend washing, chopping and freezing it because it's not available year-round.

SALO – САЛО: This Ukrainian specialty is essentially salt-cured pork fat, similar to Canadian bacon. The cured fat is thinly sliced and served as an appetizer with dark rye bread, green onions and salt. It's a traditional appetizer that's still enjoyed by many today.

ROE AND CAVIAR – ИКРА (IKRA):

Because seafood is such a large part of Eastern Europe's cuisine, it's no wonder that caviar is so popular and highly prized. When selecting salmon roe for my Smoked Salmon and Caviar Blini (page 13), make sure the beads of roe are firm and smell fresh. They should not be deflated or smell too fishy, both signs that it's been standing for a while. I also recommend trout roe and whitefish caviar—both are delicious and slightly less expensive than salmon roe or true black sturgeon caviar. Avoid anything that has been dyed black.

BUCKWHEAT – ГРЕЧИХА (GRECHIKHA):

This hearty and aromatic grain is equivalent to rice in Eastern European cuisine. It can be simply prepared with water and salt or seasoned with spices and mixed with vegetables. It can be used as a base for braised meats instead of mashed potatoes or rice and added to soups. I recommend using roasted buckwheat because it has great flavor.

AGAR GELATIN – АГАР АГАР (AGAR AGAR):

Agar gelatin is a seaweed-based vegan gelatin that is used to make Russian marshmallow, or *zefir*. This gelatin is available in Asian and Russian markets, and it can easily be found online. It cannot be substituted with regular gelatin because it sets at room temperature and sets much firmer. The recipe for Fruit Marshmallow (page 139) will work only with this type of gelatin.

PELMENI MAKER – ПЕЛЬМЕННИЦА (PELEMENITSA):

Making hundreds of pelmeni by hand can take hours, so an ingenious pelmeni maker was invented! This metal form can make up to forty pelmeni at a time, making the process a breeze. You can find one of these specialty forms at a Russian market, or you can search for it online.

CAST-IRON POT – ЧУГУННАЯ КАСТРЮЛЯ (CHUGUNNAYA KASTRYULYA):

Most Eastern European recipes for braised meat were traditionally prepared in heavy, cast-iron pots. The steady heat of cast iron is perfect for low-and-slow cooking. I recommend using a cast-iron pot (i.e., a Dutch oven) for any of my braised meat recipes.

WAFFLE MAKER – ВАФЕЛЬНИЦА (VAFEL'NYTSA):

Crispy golden waffles filled with caramel or whipped cream are very popular in Eastern Europe. For my Caramel Waffle Rolls (page 154), you'll need a waffle cone, *krumkake* or *pizzelle* maker. You can find one of these machines in specialty culinary stores or online.

UNIQUE BITES AND SMALL DISHES

This chapter is a recipe collection that would make any Eastern European drool with happiness! We are starting off with appetizers and small bites, just like any meal starts in Eastern Europe. Here, you'll find unique Slavic recipes like Smoked Salmon and Caviar Blini (page 13), Chicken and Mushroom Crepes (page 21), Zucchini "Caviar" Spread (page 26) and a variety of open-faced tea sandwiches (pages 33 and 34). Many of these recipes can also double as snacks, especially the piroshki (pages 14 to 18) and Beef and Garlic Meat Pies (page 22). In Eastern Europe, it's not unusual to have an entire meal made up of these small dishes. A typical get-together with friends and family will include these appetizers alongside a simple dessert and tea, wine, Cognac or vodka. And like a true Ukrainian, don't forget to serve salo (see page 8) with rye bread and spring onions on the side!

SMOKED SALMON AND CAVIAR BLINI

Блинчики с Икрой ✤ Blinchiki s Ikroy

You'll love the combination of velvety crème fraîche, smoked salmon and loads of salmon roe in this recipe. Caviar blini, or mini pancakes, like these are very popular in Eastern Europe and can be enjoyed with red or black caviar. They are luxurious snacks usually reserved for parties, celebrations and New Year's Eve. Make these blini for a special evening with a side of vodka or hot black tea. If you're short on time, grab some premade, store-bought mini pancakes and reheat them in your oven.

YIELD: 24 BLINI

Prepare the mini pancakes first (see Quick Tip). In a large bowl, combine the milk and vinegar. Whisk them together and let the mixture stand for 5 minutes to allow the milk to sour.

Add the egg and butter to the milk mixture and whisk for 1 minute, until smooth.

In a medium bowl, combine the flour, baking powder, baking soda and salt. Sift the flour mixture into the milk mixture and whisk until the batter is smooth.

Preheat a pancake griddle or nonstick skillet over medium heat and add a drizzle of the oil. Add about 1½ tablespoons (23 ml) of the batter per pancake to the griddle. Cook the pancakes about 1 minute on the first side, until air bubbles rise and pop on the surface. Flip the pancakes over with a spatula and cook for 30 seconds. Transfer the pancakes to a wire rack to cool.

To make the crème fraîche, combine the crème fraîche and dill in a small bowl. Spread a generous amount of the mixture on each pancake.

Top the pancakes with the smoked salmon, salmon roe and dill.

QUICK TIP: These pancakes can be prepared ahead of time and stored in an airtight container until you are ready to serve them. Store them in the refrigerator for up to 2 days and in the freezer for up to 1 month.

MINI PANCAKES

1 cup (240 ml) whole milk

1 tbsp (15 ml) white vinegar

1 large egg

2 tbsp (30 ml) melted butter

1⅓ cups (166 g) all-purpose flour

1 tsp baking powder

1 tsp baking soda

¼ tsp salt

Canola or grapeseed oil, as needed

CRÈME FRAÎCHE

½ cup (120 g) crème fraîche

3 tbsp (6 g) finely chopped fresh dill

TOPPINGS

6 oz (168 g) smoked salmon, thinly sliced

1 cup (200 g) salmon roe

Finely chopped fresh dill, as needed

BEEF AND CHEESE PIROSHKI

Пирожки с Мясом и Сыром ✤ Piroshki s Myasom i Sirom

This is my all-time favorite piroshki recipe! These iconic deep-fried pockets (the Russian version of hand pies) are packed with beef, cheese and incredible flavor. The filling is juicy and extra cheesy, thanks to the mozzarella cheese and onion. And there's a touch of dill that adds some quintessential Eastern European flavor.

YIELD: 16 PIROSHKI

To make the yeast dough, whisk the milk and sugar together in a large bowl, then sprinkle in the dry yeast. Allow it to proof for 5 minutes. Next, add the salt, butter and egg, whisking for about 2 minutes. Begin mixing the flour in, in ½-cup (63-g) increments, until a soft dough forms. Transfer it to a lightly floured work surface and knead for 4 to 5 minutes, until the dough is smooth and uniform. Place it into a large bowl, cover it with a towel and allow it to proof for 1 hour, or until doubled in size.

While the dough is proofing, preheat a large skillet over medium heat and melt the butter in the skillet. Add the beef and fry for 5 to 6 minutes, breaking it into pieces along the way with a spatula, until well browned and cooked through. Remove from the heat and allow the beef to cool.

Grate the onion into a large bowl and add the mozzarella, dill, salt, black pepper and garlic powder. Add the cooled beef and mix everything together.

Once the dough has proofed, assemble the piroshki. Heat the oil in a large pot with tall sides over medium heat until the oil reaches 350°F (177°C).

Dust a work surface with flour. Divide the dough into 16 equal pieces. Roll each piece into a 5-inch (13-cm) circle with a rolling pin. Add ¼ cup (60 g) of the filling to the center of the circle. Starting from the middle, bring the edges of the dough up over the filling and pinch it at the top, then continue pinching along the edges until secure.

Assemble and fry the piroshki in small batches, 3 to 4 at a time, and do not let them sit for too long once they are assembled. Fry the piroshki for about 5 minutes, rotating them every minute to brown them evenly. Transfer the piroshki onto a wire rack lined with paper towels to absorb the excess oil. These piroshki are best enjoyed warm.

YEAST DOUGH

1½ cups (360 ml) lukewarm whole milk

1 tbsp (13 g) sugar

1 tbsp (9 g) active dry yeast

1 tsp salt

¼ cup (56 g) butter, melted

1 large egg

4 cups (500 g) all-purpose flour

BEEF AND CHEESE FILLING

1 tbsp (14 g) butter

1 lb (450 g) 85% lean ground beef

1 large onion

2½ cups (250 g) grated mozzarella cheese

1 tbsp (2 g) finely chopped fresh dill

2 tsp (10 g) salt

1 tsp ground black pepper

1 tsp garlic powder

FOR FRYING

6 to 8 cups (1.4 to 1.9 L) canola or grapeseed oil

COTTAGE CHEESE AND DILL PIROSHKI

Пирожки с Сыром ✤ Piroshki s Sirom

These surprisingly simple cheesy piroshki are made with tvorog *(quark) or cottage cheese, dill and green onions. This piroshki recipe is one of our family favorites—my mom always made a huge batch of them because they would be gone in minutes! They store very well—just cool and refrigerate any leftovers for a tasty snack anytime.*

YIELD: 16 PIROSHKI

To make the yeast dough, whisk the milk and sugar together in a large bowl for 1 minute. Sprinkle the dry yeast over the top and allow it to proof for 5 minutes. Next, whisk in the salt, butter and egg until smooth. Begin mixing in the flour in ½-cup (63-g) increments, until a soft dough forms. Transfer to a lightly floured work surface and knead the dough for 4 to 5 minutes, until it is very smooth and uniform. Place the dough into a large bowl, cover it with a towel and allow it to proof for 1 hour, or until it has doubled in size.

Meanwhile, line a large, fine-mesh strainer with cheesecloth and add the cottage cheese. Rinse the cheese with cold water until just the curds remain. Wring out as much water as possible, until the cheese curds are crumbly. Place the cheese into a large bowl and add the dill, egg and egg yolk, green onions, salt and black pepper. Mix all the ingredients together.

Once the dough has proofed, assemble and fry the piroshki. Heat the oil in a deep sauté pan over medium heat until the oil reaches 350°F (177°C).

Dust a work surface with flour. Divide the dough into 16 equal pieces. For each piroshok, roll the dough into a 5-inch (13-cm) circle using a rolling pin. Add ⅓ cup (80 g) of the filling to the center of the circle, forming a half moon. Starting from the middle, bring the edges of the dough up over the filling and pinch it at the top, then continue pinching along the edges until secure.

Assemble and fry the piroshki in small batches, 3 to 4 piroshki at a time. Fry for about 5 minutes, rotating the piroshki every minute to brown them evenly. Transfer the piroshki to a wire rack lined with paper towels to absorb the excess oil. They are best enjoyed warm.

YEAST DOUGH

1½ cups (360 ml) lukewarm whole milk

1 tbsp (13 g) sugar

1½ tbsp (14 g) active dry yeast

1 tsp salt

¼ cup (56 g) butter, melted

1 large egg

4 cups (500 g) all-purpose flour

CHEESE FILLING

3 lbs (1.4 kg) large-curd cottage cheese

2 tbsp (4 g) finely chopped fresh dill

1 large egg plus 1 large egg yolk

2 green onions, diced

2 tsp (10 g) salt

½ tsp ground black pepper

FOR FRYING

2 cups (480 ml) canola or grapeseed oil

BRAISED CABBAGE AND MUSHROOM PIROSHKI

Пирожки с Капустой ✤ Piroshki s Kapustoy

This is the most special and nostalgic piroshki recipe for me. My grandmother was famous for her cabbage-stuffed piroshki. Her secret ingredient? Sauerkraut. When I make these now, I feel like I've been transported back to her tiny kitchen, where we waited patiently for the piroshki to finish frying. For my version of this classic recipe, I also like to add bell peppers, mushrooms, carrots and smoked sausage.

YIELD: 16 PIROSHKI

To make the yeast dough, whisk the milk and sugar in a large bowl for 1 minute. Sprinkle the dry yeast over the top and allow it to proof for 5 minutes. Next, whisk in the salt, butter and egg until smooth. Begin mixing in the flour in ½-cup (63-g) increments, until a soft dough forms. Transfer the dough to a lightly floured work surface and knead for 4 to 5 minutes, until very smooth and uniform. Place the dough into a large bowl, cover it with a towel and allow it to proof for 1 hour, or until it has doubled in size.

Meanwhile, preheat a large sauté pan over medium heat and melt the butter. Add the bell pepper, mushrooms and onion. Add the sausage (if using). Sauté for 5 to 6 minutes, until the vegetables are tender but not browned. Add the garlic and cook for 1 minute. Add the cabbage, sauerkraut, carrot, salt, black pepper and paprika. Toss all the ingredients together, then cover the pan with a lid and reduce the heat to low. Braise the filling for 20 to 25 minutes, tossing every 5 minutes, until the cabbage is wilted and tender. Remove the braised cabbage filling from the heat and stir in the fresh dill.

Once the dough has proofed, assemble the piroshki. Heat the oil in a large pot with tall sides over medium heat until it reaches 350°F (177°C).

Dust a work surface with flour. Divide the dough into 16 equal pieces. For each piroshok, roll the dough into a 5-inch (13-cm) circle using a rolling pin. Add ⅓ to ½ cup (80 to 120 g) of the filling to the center of the circle, forming a half moon. Starting from the middle, bring the edges of the dough up over the filling and pinch it at the top, then continue pinching along the edges until secure.

Assemble and fry the piroshki in small batches, 3 to 4 piroshki at a time. Fry the piroshki for about 5 minutes, rotating every minute to brown them evenly. Transfer the piroshki to a wire rack lined with paper towels to absorb the excess oil. They are best enjoyed warm.

YEAST DOUGH

1½ cups (360 ml) lukewarm whole milk

1 tbsp (13 g) sugar

1 tbsp (9 g) active dry yeast

1 tsp salt

¼ cup (56 g) butter, melted

1 large egg

4 cups (500 g) all-purpose flour

CABBAGE AND MUSHROOM FILLING

2 tbsp (28 g) butter

1 large red bell pepper, diced

6 to 8 white mushrooms, diced

1 medium onion, diced

1 cup (140 g) diced smoked sausage (optional)

4 cloves garlic, minced

1 small head cabbage, shredded

½ cup (75 g) sauerkraut

1 large carrot, grated

1½ tsp (8 g) salt

Ground black pepper, as needed

1 tsp paprika

1 tbsp (2 g) finely chopped fresh dill

FOR FRYING

6 to 8 cups (1.4 to 1.9 L) canola or grapeseed oil

CHICKEN AND MUSHROOM CREPES

Блинчики с Грибами ✤ Blinchiki s Gribami

Crepes of all kinds can be found in Eastern Europe and not only with caviar! These savory dill crepes are stuffed with a chicken-mushroom mixture and served warm with sour cream. I also like to add some cheese to the filling to give it even more flavor.

YIELD: 15 CREPES

To make the crepes, combine the eggs, milk, butter, salt, dill and flour in a blender. Pulse for 2 minutes, until a smooth batter forms. Or you can whisk the batter in a large bowl by hand. Gradually sift in the flour, whisking after each addition. Whisk for about 1 minute, until the batter is free of clumps.

Preheat an 8-inch (20-cm) crepe pan or medium nonstick skillet over medium heat. Pour ¼ cup (60 ml) of the batter into the center of the pan, then tilt the pan around in a circular motion until the batter spreads evenly across it. Cook the crepe for approximately 1 minute on the first side. Turn it when the edges start turning golden brown. Cook the second side for 30 seconds. Stack the crepes on a wire rack to cool.

To make the filling, preheat a large skillet over medium-high heat and add 1 tablespoon (14 g) of the butter. Once the butter is hot, add the chicken and season it with 1 teaspoon of the salt and the ¼ teaspoon of black pepper. Fry the chicken until it's browned and cooked through, about 5 minutes. Transfer the chicken to a large bowl and set it aside.

In the same skillet, melt 2 tablespoons (28 g) of the butter over medium heat. Add the mushrooms and onion. Sauté until the mushrooms are golden and the onion is tender, about 6 to 7 minutes. During the last minute, add the garlic and stir. Season the mixture with the remaining ½ teaspoon salt, coriander, cumin and black pepper to taste. Transfer to the bowl of chicken, then add the mozzarella cheese and dill. Stir until the mixture is uniform.

To fill the crepes, place approximately ⅓ cup (80 g) of the filling into the center of the crepe. Fold over the sides of the crepe and roll tightly, forming an egg-roll shape. Place the stuffed crepes into a large baking dish and transfer it to the refrigerator if you are not serving the crepes right away.

Preheat a large skillet over medium heat and add 2 tablespoons (28 g) of the butter. Place 4 to 5 crepes, seam side down, into the skillet. Cook the crepes for 3 minutes per side, or until they are golden brown. Add the remaining 3 tablespoons (42 g) butter to the skillet as needed to cook the rest of the crepes. Serve the crepes warm with the sour cream.

CREPES

4 large eggs

2 cups (480 ml) milk

¼ cup (56 g) butter, melted

½ tsp salt

1 tbsp (2 g) finely chopped fresh dill

1⅔ cups (208 g) all-purpose flour

FILLING

½ cup (112 g) butter, divided

1 lb (450 g) ground chicken or turkey

1½ tsp (8 g) salt, divided

¼ tsp ground black pepper, plus more to taste

15 white mushrooms, thinly sliced

1 medium onion, diced

4 cloves garlic, minced

½ tsp ground coriander

½ tsp ground cumin

1 cup (100 g) grated mozzarella cheese

2 tbsp (4 g) finely chopped fresh dill

FOR SERVING

Sour cream, as needed

QUICK TIP: To reheat leftover crepes, preheat a medium skillet over medium heat and add 1 tablespoon (14 g) of butter. Once the butter has melted, add the crepes and fry them over medium heat for 4 to 5 minutes, turning every minute to reheat them evenly.

BEEF AND GARLIC MEAT PIES

Чебуреки ✦ Cheboureki

I can't say enough about how delicious, succulent and flavorful these meat pies, or cheboureki, are. They are the ultimate Eastern European street food. These snacks are made with a simple dough that becomes crispy and flaky when deep-fried. The filling, made with ground beef or pork and loads of onion, is so juicy. The grated onion adds all the moisture the filling needs.

YIELD: 8 LARGE CHEBOUREKI OR 16 SMALL CHEBOUREKI

To make the dough, whisk together the water, oil and salt in a large bowl. Gradually stir in the flour with a wooden spoon or spatula. Mix the ingredients well after each addition. Once all the flour is added, transfer the dough to a lightly floured work surface. Knead the dough for 4 to 5 minutes, until it's elastic and smooth. (It needs to be firm and not sticky; add more flour if necessary.) Cover the dough with plastic wrap and chill it in the refrigerator for at least 30 minutes. The dough can be prepared the day before.

To make the filling, place the beef into a large bowl. Grate the onion into the bowl, then add the garlic, salt, black pepper, dill and parsley. Use a spatula to combine the ingredients, until the mixture is uniform.

Once the dough has rested, knead it again for 1 minute, then use a sharp knife to divide the dough into 8 pieces for large meat pies or into 16 pieces for smaller pies.

For each meat pie, roll the dough out into a circle on a lightly floured work surface until it is very thin and almost transparent: 8 inches (20 cm) in diameter for larger cheboureki and 5 inches (13 cm) in diameter for smaller cheboureki.

Place the filling—½ cup (120 g) for large cheboureki or ¼ cup (60 g) for small cheboureki—onto one half of the dough circle, flattening and spreading the filling to within ½ inch (13 mm) of the edge. Fold the other half of the dough over the filling, then use a fork to seal the dough tightly.

Heat the oil in a large sauté pan over medium heat until the oil reaches 300°F (148°C). Fry 2 to 3 meat pies at a time for 3 to 4 minutes per side, until they are golden brown and crispy. Transfer the meat pies to a wire rack lined with paper towels to absorb any excess oil.

Serve the cheboureki while they are still warm. Keep leftovers refrigerated and bake them for 5 minutes in an oven preheated to 425°F (218°C).

DOUGH

1 cup (240 ml) water

½ cup (120 ml) canola or grapeseed oil

1 tsp salt

4 cups (500 g) all-purpose flour

FILLING

1 lb (450 g) 85% lean ground beef

1 medium onion

4 to 5 cloves garlic, pressed

2 tsp (10 g) salt

1 tsp ground black pepper

1 tbsp (2 g) finely chopped fresh dill

1 tbsp (2 g) finely chopped fresh parsley or cilantro

FOR FRYING

3 to 4 cups (720 to 960 ml) canola or grapeseed oil

SMOKED SALMON CHEESE PANCAKES

Сырники с Лососем ✤ Sirniki s Lososom

These savory cheese pancakes are the perfect way to start a meal, or they can be enjoyed as a snack. They're made with sautéed onion, smoked salmon and dill, then served with sour cream and more smoked salmon. This easy appetizer recipe is typically made with quark cheese, which I have substituted with cottage cheese. Using farina for this recipe keeps the pancakes together and also keeps them very light and fluffy.

YIELD: 18 TO 20 PANCAKES

3 lbs (1.4 kg) large-curd cottage cheese

1 tsp salt

1 large egg plus 1 large egg yolk

⅓ cup (60 g) farina

1 tbsp (14 g) butter

1 small onion, diced

5 oz (140 g) smoked salmon, plus more as needed (optional)

2 tbsp (4 g) finely fresh dill

Canola or grapeseed oil, as needed

½ cup (120 g) sour cream

Line a large, fine-mesh strainer with cheesecloth and add the cottage cheese. Rinse the cheese with cold water until just the curds remain. Once the liquids have drained, carefully lift the cheesecloth out of the strainer and wring the cheese to remove as much liquid as possible.

Transfer the cheese to a large bowl and add the salt, egg and egg yolk and farina. Use a spatula to combine the ingredients. Cover the bowl with plastic wrap and place it into the refrigerator for at least 15 minutes to allow the farina to soften and bloom.

Meanwhile, preheat a medium skillet over medium heat and melt the butter. Add the onion and sauté for 3 to 4 minutes, until the onion is translucent but not browned.

Remove the salmon from its packaging and dice it into pea-sized pieces. Once the farina has bloomed, add the dill, salmon and onion to the cheese mixture and stir until the mixture is uniform.

Use a small scoop to measure about 1 ½ tablespoons (23 g) per pancake. Roll the scoop of the cheese mixture into a ball, then gently flatten it into a disk.

Preheat a large skillet over medium-low heat and add 2 tablespoons (30 ml) of oil. Fry the pancakes for 2 to 3 minutes per side, until they are golden brown. Transfer the pancakes to a tray lined with paper towels to absorb the excess oil.

Serve the pancakes warm with a dollop of the sour cream on top and more salmon (if using).

ZUCCHINI "CAVIAR" SPREAD

Кабачковая Икра ✤ Kabachkovaya Ikra

This easy and delicious eggplant spread is made with tons of veggies, which makes it great for summertime! The braised bell pepper, carrots and eggplant come together to create an unforgettable medley of flavors. My mom always made this spread with the extra eggplants and zucchini from our garden. I love to use this spread for sandwiches and as a warm dip for rustic bread. The spread will keep in the refrigerator for up to a week, so you'll have plenty of time to enjoy it.

YIELD: 4 CUPS (960 G)

Preheat a large sauté pan over medium-high heat. Add the butter and allow it to melt. Add the onion, bell pepper and carrots. Sauté this mixture for 5 to 7 minutes, until the onions are soft but not brown.

Add the zucchini, eggplant and tomatoes. Add the salt, black pepper, smoked paprika, garlic powder and sugar (if using). Cover the sauté pan and reduce the heat to medium-low. Cook the mixture for 30 minutes, stirring every 5 minutes.

Once the vegetables are tender, remove the sauté pan from the heat and allow the vegetables to cool slightly. When they have cooled, transfer the mixture to a blender or food processor and pulse until a smooth puree forms. Allow the spread to cool before transferring it to glass jars and storing it in the refrigerator for up to 1 week. When serving, garnish the spread with a sprinkle of fresh dill.

¼ cup (56 g) salted butter

1 medium sweet onion, diced

1 medium red bell pepper, diced

3 medium carrots, diced

3 to 4 medium zucchini, diced

1 large eggplant, peeled and cubed

2 medium tomatoes, seeded and diced

1½ tsp (8 g) salt

Ground black pepper, as needed

½ tsp smoked paprika

½ tsp garlic powder

1 tsp sugar (optional)

1 tbsp (2 g) finely chopped fresh dill

JUICY BEEF CUTLETS

Говяжьи Котлеты ✤ Govyazh'i Kotleti

Cutlets of all kinds are enjoyed in Eastern Europe for lunch, dinner and snack time. These inexpensive meat patties are easy to make and can employ a variety of meats, such as chicken, pork, beef or even fish. This version, made with ground beef, is juicy and flavorful and can be enjoyed on its own with sliced bread or as a side with pasta, potatoes and gravy or salad. I recommend using 85 percent lean ground beef—the extra fat gives the recipe both flavor and moisture.

YIELD: ABOUT 15 CUTLETS

Break the bread into large chunks and soak the pieces in water for 2 to 3 minutes. Using your hands, gently press the water out of the bread.

Transfer the bread to a large bowl. Add the beef, onion, egg, dill, parsley, salt and black pepper. Use your hands or a spatula to mix the ingredients thoroughly, until the mixture is uniform.

Place the breadcrumbs in a shallow dish. Use a ¼-cup (60-g) measuring cup to scoop out the portion for each cutlet. Roll the meat into a ball, then roll the ball in the breadcrumbs until it is well coated. Flatten the ball slightly and place it on a tray until you are ready to fry.

Preheat a large skillet over medium heat and add 2 tablespoons (30 ml) of the oil. Fry the cutlets in batches, 5 to 8 cutlets at a time, to avoid overcrowding the skillet. Add the remaining 2 tablespoons (30 ml) of oil as needed. Fry the cutlets for 4 to 5 minutes per side, turning after the first side is golden brown. During the last 2 to 3 minutes of cooking time, cover the skillet to steam the cutlets slightly. Transfer the cutlets to a tray lined with paper towels to remove excess oil.

1 (3-inch [8-cm]) thick slice day-old French bread

1 lb (450 g) 85% lean ground beef

1 large onion, grated

1 large egg

1 tbsp (2 g) finely chopped fresh dill

1 tbsp (2 g) finely chopped fresh parsley

1½ tsp (8 g) salt

1 tsp ground black pepper

1 cup (50 g) panko breadcrumbs

¼ cup (60 ml) canola or grapeseed oil, divided

CHICKEN EGG ROULADE

Рулет из Омлета с Фаршем ❋ Roulet iz Omletta s Farshom

I love everything about this incredibly delicious recipe! This traditional, delicate chicken roulade is made with an omelet-like outside and a juicy meat filling inside. Once baked, it's thinly sliced and served either as an appetizer with bread and sour cream or as the meat entrée for dinner alongside pasta or mashed potatoes. I like to make the meat filling with ground chicken or turkey so it doesn't overwhelm the other flavors, but pork or beef will also work well. Look for ground meat with a higher fat content for a juicier filling.

YIELD: 5 TO 6 SERVINGS

Preheat the oven to 350°F (177°C). Line a 9 x 13–inch (23 x 33–cm) jelly roll pan with parchment paper and set it aside.

To make the omelet, preheat a small skillet over medium heat. Add the butter and allow it to melt. Add the shallot and sauté for 3 to 4 minutes, until the shallot is translucent. Remove the skillet from the heat and let the shallot cool.

In a large bowl, combine the sour cream, eggs, parsley, dill, salt, black pepper and paprika. Whisk for 1 to 2 minutes, until the eggs are smooth. Add the mozzarella cheese and shallot. Whisk again for 1 minute, until the mixture is uniform. Pour the mixture onto the prepared jelly roll pan. Use a spatula to spread the cheese and egg in an even layer.

Bake the omelet for 10 minutes, until it is just set.

While the omelet is baking, prepare the meat filling. Combine the chicken, egg, salt, black pepper, parsley, dill and coriander in a large bowl. Grate the onion into the mixture, then use a spatula to gently stir everything together.

Drop spoonfuls of the meat filling onto the baked omelet, then use an offset spatula to spread the meat filling evenly to the edges of the omelet. Using the parchment paper to help you, gently roll the omelet and meat filling into a log, starting from the short side of the pan. Roll the roulade tightly but gently.

Place the roulade back onto the parchment paper and cover it lightly with foil. Bake it for 30 minutes. Remove the foil and bake for 15 minutes. Remove the roulade from the oven and let it cool for at least 15 minutes before using a sharp, serrated knife to slice the roll thinly. Serve the roulade warm with sour cream on the side.

OMELET

1 tbsp (14 g) butter

1 medium shallot, diced

¼ cup (60 g) sour cream

4 large eggs

1 tbsp (2 g) finely chopped fresh parsley

1 tbsp (2 g) finely chopped fresh dill

½ tsp salt

¼ tsp ground black pepper

¼ tsp paprika

1½ cups (150 g) grated mozzarella cheese

MEAT FILLING

1 lb (450 g) ground chicken or turkey

1 large egg

1 tsp salt

¼ tsp ground black pepper

1 tbsp (2 g) finely chopped fresh parsley

1 tbsp (2 g) finely chopped fresh dill

¼ tsp ground coriander

1 small onion

FOR SERVING

Sour cream, as needed

SPRAT AND TOMATO TEA SANDWICH

Бутерброды с Шпротами ❖ Booterbrod s Shprotami

This unique seafood tea sandwich is one of my husband's favorites! These small bites are made with dark bread, garlic mayonnaise, tomatoes, a sprinkle of dill and canned sprats. The little fish are very popular in Eastern Europe and enjoyed plain, on sandwiches and in salads. I recommend going with sprats marinated in oil, as they work best for this recipe. You may need to head to a Russian grocery store to find them.

YIELD: 20 TEA SANDWICHES

½ cup (110 g) mayonnaise

5 cloves garlic, pressed or minced

2 tbsp (4 g) finely chopped fresh dill, plus more as needed

1 baguette or rye cocktail bread, thinly sliced

4 to 5 medium Roma tomatoes, thinly sliced

1 (8-oz [224-g]) can sprats in oil

Salt, as needed

Combine the mayonnaise, garlic and dill in a small bowl and stir for 1 minute.

To assemble the sandwiches, spread a generous amount of the garlic mayonnaise onto the baguette slices, followed by 1 slice of tomato and 1 to 2 sprats. Season the sandwiches lightly with salt and garnish with additional dill. Serve the sandwiches immediately.

CREAMY CARROT TEA SANDWICH

Бутерброды с Морковью ✦ Booterbrod s Morkov'yu

Teatime is a serious event in Eastern Europe and always includes small appetizers and a variety of tea sandwiches just like these simple, open-faced sandwiches, made with a creamy carrot spread consisting of carrots, cheese, onion and garlic. The spread itself can be made ahead of time and stored in the refrigerator for up to three days. When you're ready to enjoy the spread, just smear it on sliced bread and toast the sandwich in the oven.

YIELD: ABOUT 25 SANDWICHES

Preheat the oven to 425°F (218°C).

Preheat a large sauté pan over medium heat and add the butter. Once the butter has melted, add the carrots and onion and sauté for 6 to 7 minutes, until the carrots are tender but not browned. Remove this mixture from the heat and let it cool.

Meanwhile, in a large bowl, combine the mozzarella cheese, cream cheese, mayonnaise, garlic, salt, smoked paprika, black pepper, 1 tablespoon (2 g) of the parsley and the dill. Once the carrot and onion mixture has cooled, add it to the bowl. Use a spatula to fold everything together, creating a uniform spread.

Spread a heaping amount of the carrot mixture onto the baguette slices and place on a large baking sheet. Bake the sandwiches for 15 to 17 minutes, until the bread is toasted. Remove the sandwiches from the oven, garnish them with the remaining 1 tablespoon (2 g) of parsley and serve them warm.

2 tbsp (28 g) butter

4 large carrots, grated

1 small onion, diced

½ cup (50 g) grated mozzarella cheese

½ cup (120 g) cream cheese, softened

½ cup (110 g) mayonnaise

4 cloves garlic, pressed

1 tsp salt

½ tsp smoked paprika

¼ tsp ground black pepper

2 tbsp (4 g) finely chopped fresh parsley, divided

1 tbsp (2 g) finely chopped fresh dill

1 large baguette, thinly sliced

STUFFED POTATO PANCAKES

Драники ✦ Draniki

If you enjoy latkes, you're going to love this recipe: stuffed potato pancakes that boast a juicy meat filling. Potato pancakes have always been popular in Eastern Europe, so it's no surprise that there are many different variations. I love to enjoy these while they're still hot with a nice dollop of sour cream on top.

YIELD: 20 TO 25 PANCAKES

To make the filling, combine the beef, dill, parsley, salt and black pepper in a large bowl. Grate the onion into the bowl, then use a spatula to fold everything together. Use a 1-tablespoon (15-g) scoop to measure out the meat for each pancake. Flatten the meat into small patties, slightly smaller than what you want the pancakes to be. Set the patties on a tray and set the tray aside.

To make the potato pancakes, grate the potatoes into a large bowl. Add the onion, flour, egg, salt and black pepper. Use a whisk or spatula to stir the ingredients together for about 1 minute.

Preheat a large skillet (or two) over medium heat and add 2 tablespoons (30 ml) of the oil. To shape the pancakes, add 1 heaping tablespoon (18 g) of the potato mixture to the skillet, top the potato mixture with a meat patty and then seal the filling inside with 1 heaping tablespoon (18 g) of potato mixture on top. Fry the pancakes about 3 to 4 minutes per side, turning once the potatoes are golden brown. Add more oil as needed.

Meanwhile, preheat the oven to 425°F (218°C). Line a large baking sheet with parchment paper or a silicone mat.

As the pancakes finish frying, place them onto the prepared baking sheet. Once all the pancakes have finished frying, bake the pancakes for 10 to 15 minutes, until the internal temperature of the meat reaches 160°F (71°C). Remove the pancakes from the oven and serve them hot with the sour cream.

FILLING

1 lb (450 g) 85% lean ground beef

1 tbsp (2 g) finely chopped fresh dill

1 tbsp (2 g) finely chopped fresh parsley

1 tsp salt

½ tsp ground black pepper

1 medium onion

POTATO PANCAKES

6 large russet potatoes, peeled

1 large onion, grated

⅔ cup (83 g) all-purpose flour

1 large egg

2 tsp (10 g) salt

½ tsp ground black pepper

FOR FRYING AND SERVING

2 tbsp (30 ml) canola or grapeseed oil, plus more as needed

Sour cream, as needed

COMFORT FOODS AND MEATY MAIN ENTRÉES

This chapter has all the hearty and warming entrées that are essential to Ukrainian and Eastern European cuisine. These meaty and flavor-packed recipes are the comfort foods of Slavic culture. From Stewed Beef and Potatoes (page 54) to Pelmeni (page 42) to Chicken Kiev (page 63), you'll find all your comforting dishes here. Hungry for pasta? Enjoy the Navy-Style Pasta with Beef (page 64). Looking for a flavorful rice dish? Try the Beef and Garlic Rice Pilaf (page 53), made with loads of beef seasoned with garlic and cumin. And you can never go wrong with Beef and Mushroom Cabbage Rolls (page 58). Whichever dish you make, it's bound to satisfy any comfort-food craving!

BRAISED PORK WITH GRAVY

Тушеное Мясо с Картошкой ❦ Tooshonoye Myaso s Kartoshkoy

A delicious, aromatic and inexpensive meat dish, this is a traditional Ukrainian recipe. As you look through this cookbook, you'll notice the recipes don't call for expensive cuts of meat; that's because they weren't (and still aren't) readily available in Eastern Europe. Recipes like this braised pork are very common because they utilize the cheaper cuts of meat without compromising on flavor. Enjoy the melt-in-your-mouth braised pork with my Butter and Sour Cream Mashed Potatoes (page 94) and a refreshing salad on the side.

This recipe can be prepared using a slow cooker, a pressure cooker or the stove. If using a pressure cooker or slow cooker, prepare the recipe according to the instructions but reduce the amount of water to 1½ cups (360 ml).

YIELD: 6 SERVINGS

6 tbsp (90 ml) grapeseed oil, divided

2 lbs (900 g) pork shoulder, cut into 1½- to 2-inch (4- to 5-cm) pieces

2 large carrots, diced

1 large sweet onion, diced

2 to 3 cloves garlic, minced

2 tsp (10 g) salt

1 tsp ground black pepper

¼ tsp ground cumin

¼ tsp ground coriander

¼ tsp paprika

2 cups (480 ml) water

2 tbsp (30 g) ketchup

2 tbsp (30 g) sour cream

1 batch Butter and Sour Cream Mashed Potatoes (page 94)

Finely chopped fresh dill, as needed

Finely chopped fresh parsley, as needed

Preheat a large braising pan over medium-high heat and add 2 tablespoons (30 ml) of the oil. Add half of the pork and fry until it is well browned all over, about 7 minutes. Transfer the pork to a large bowl, add 2 tablespoons (30 ml) of the oil to the braising pan and repeat this process with the other half of the pork. Set the cooked pork aside.

Reduce the heat to medium and add the remaining 2 tablespoons (30 ml) of oil. Add the carrots, onion and garlic. Sauté this mixture until the onion is translucent but not brown, about 5 minutes. Return the pork to the braising pan and stir to combine. Season the mixture with the salt, black pepper, cumin, coriander and paprika.

In a medium measuring cup, combine the water, ketchup and sour cream, whisking until the mixture is smooth. Pour the mixture into the braising pan and stir to combine.

Allow the sauce to come to a simmer, then cover the braising pan, reduce the heat to low and cook for 1½ hours (if you are cooking on the stove), stirring occasionally. If you are using a pressure cooker, cook for 25 to 30 minutes under high pressure (or use the Meat setting for programmable pressure cookers). If you are using a slow cooker, cook on high for 5 hours, or until the meat is very tender.

To serve, ladle a generous amount of meat and sauce over a bed of the Butter and Sour Cream Mashed Potatoes and garnish each serving with the dill and parsley.

PELMENI

Пелмени ✤ Pelmeni

These famous Russian meat dumplings can boast a variety of fillings—pork, beef, veal and even chicken. They are popular across Eastern Europe and can easily be purchased at a specialty Russian store, but that wouldn't be any fun. Homemade pelmeni really are the best. I've included two different methods of dressing the pelmeni in this recipe: one with caramelized onion and one with sour cream and vinegar. Either one is delicious!

To learn how to freeze the pelmeni or make them with a pelmeni maker, see the Quick Tips following the recipe.

YIELD: 80 PELMENI

To make the dumplings, combine the eggs, water and salt in a large bowl. Whisk the ingredients together for 1 minute, until the mixture is smooth. Gradually add the flour, stirring after each addition, to create a firm dough ball. Transfer the dough to a generously floured work surface and knead it for 4 to 5 minutes, until it's smooth and elastic.

Cover the dough with plastic wrap and place it in the refrigerator to rest for at least an hour. The dough can be prepared up to 2 days in advance. Store it, covered, in the refrigerator.

To make the filling, place the beef in a large bowl. Add the garlic, salt, black pepper, coriander, cumin and dill. Grate the onion into the bowl, then use a spatula to fold everything together, creating a uniform mixture.

Lightly dust a work surface and a large baking sheet with flour. Set the baking sheet aside.

Divide the dough into 2 or 3 pieces. Roll out the dough on the floured work surface until it is about $\frac{1}{16}$ inch (2 mm) thick. Use a 1½-inch (4-cm) round cookie cutter to cut out circles for each dumpling. Place approximately 1 teaspoon of the filling in the center of each dough circle.

(Continued)

DUMPLINGS

2 large eggs

1⅓ cups (320 ml) cold water

½ tsp salt

5 cups (625 g) all-purpose flour

FILLING

1 lb (450 g) ground beef, pork or chicken

3 to 4 cloves garlic, minced

2 tsp (10 g) salt

1 tsp ground black pepper

¼ tsp ground coriander

¼ tsp ground cumin

1 tbsp (2 g) finely chopped fresh dill

1 large onion

PELMENI (CONTINUED)

To shape the dumplings, gently pull the dough up and around the filling, pinching the dough into a half-circle and sealing the filling inside. Next, pinch the two ends of the dumpling together, forming a circle. Place the shaped dumplings on the prepared baking sheet.

To cook the dumplings, bring a large pot of salted water to a rolling boil over high heat. Add 20 to 30 dumplings at a time (do not overcrowd the pot). Cook the dumplings for 5 to 6 minutes; they will float to the top as they finish cooking. Remove them with a slotted spoon and transfer them to a clean large bowl.

To make the first dressing option, the caramelized onion dressing, preheat a large skillet over medium heat and add the butter. Add the onion and sauté it for 5 to 6 minutes, until it's tender and caramelized. Add the cooked dumplings and toss to coat them in the butter and onion. Sauté the dumplings for 1 to 2 minutes to caramelize them. Season them with the salt and black pepper and garnish them with the dill.

To make the other dressing option, the sour cream and vinegar dressing, whisk together the sour cream, vinegar and dill in a large bowl for 1 minute. Add the cooked dumplings and season them with the salt and black pepper. Use a spatula to toss the dumplings until they're well coated in the dressing.

QUICK TIPS: To freeze the pelmeni, lay the shaped dumplings on a lightly floured large baking sheet and place it into the freezer overnight. Once the pelmeni are frozen, transfer them to a freezer storage bag; they will keep well for 6 months. When cooking frozen pelmeni, increase the cooking time to 10 minutes.

To make the pelmeni using a pelmeni maker, dust it lightly with flour and divide the dough into 4 to 6 pieces. On a lightly floured work surface, roll out the dough until it is about $\frac{1}{16}$ inch (2 mm) thick and a few inches larger than the form. Lay the dough over the top of the pelmeni maker. Place a small amount of the filling for each dumpling onto the dough. Cover the filling with another sheet of dough, then firmly roll a rolling pin over the top, sealing the filling inside. The dumplings will drop out of the other side of the pelmeni maker. Dough scraps can be reused.

CARAMELIZED ONION DRESSING

¼ cup (56 g) butter

1 large onion, diced

Salt, as needed

Ground black pepper, as needed

2 tbsp (4 g) finely chopped fresh dill

SOUR CREAM AND VINEGAR DRESSING

½ cup (120 g) sour cream

¼ cup (60 ml) distilled white vinegar

2 tbsp (4 g) finely chopped fresh dill

Salt, as needed

Ground black pepper, as needed

SALMON COULIBIAC

Кулебяка ✤ Kulebyaka

This old-world Russian recipe can be traced back to the 1850s, when it was made popular by Auguste Escoffier. This salmon version of beef Wellington is a true specialty dish, typically only made for special occasions because it does take some time and patience. This seafood pastry is made with flaky puff pastry stuffed with mushroom rice, lemon and herb-seasoned salmon and eggs and served with a zesty lemon sauce.

YIELD: 6 SERVINGS

To make the mushroom rice, preheat a large skillet over medium heat and melt the butter. Add the mushrooms and onion and cook for 5 to 7 minutes, until the onion is translucent. Add the garlic and sauté for 1 minute.

In a large bowl, combine the rice, mushroom mixture, salt, black pepper, coriander, cumin, dill and parsley. Use a spatula to fold the ingredients together until the mushroom rice is uniform. Set the mushroom rice aside.

To make the salmon spread, combine the butter, salt, lemon zest, dill and smoked paprika in a small bowl. Mix until the salmon spread is uniform, about 1 minute.

To make the salmon, use a sharp knife to remove the skin and any bones. Trim the tail end and sides of the salmon to make the fillet evenly sized. Pat the salmon dry with a paper towel, then spread the salmon spread evenly all over the fillet.

Preheat the oven to 375°F (191°C). Line a large baking sheet with parchment paper or a silicone mat.

Begin assembling the pastry. Roll out the first sheet of puff pastry into a 10 x 15–inch (25 x 38–cm) rectangle. Transfer it to the prepared baking sheet. Spread 1 cup (240 g) of the mushroom rice onto the center of the pastry sheet, making sure the rice covers enough area to create a bed for the salmon fillet. Place the salmon on top of the rice, then top the fish with a layer of sliced hard-boiled eggs.

(Continued)

MUSHROOM RICE

2 tbsp (28 g) butter

15 white mushrooms, thinly sliced

1 medium onion, diced

4 cloves garlic, minced

1 cup (180 g) white rice, cooked

1 tsp salt

Ground black pepper, as needed

½ tsp ground coriander

½ tsp ground cumin

1 tbsp (2 g) finely chopped fresh dill

1 tbsp (2 g) finely chopped fresh parsley

SALMON SPREAD

½ cup (112 g) butter, softened

1 tsp salt

Zest of 1 lemon

2 tbsp (4 g) finely chopped fresh dill

½ tsp smoked paprika

SALMON

1 (2-lb [900-g]) salmon fillet

3 sheets frozen puff pastry, thawed

3 large hard-boiled eggs, thickly sliced

SALMON COULIBIAC (CONTINUED)

Top the salmon with the remaining mushroom rice, forming and gently pressing it into a dome shape. Roll out the second sheet of puff pastry to the same dimensions as the first. Brush the beaten egg around the salmon and rice, then add the second layer of pastry. Use a fork to press the two layers together, sealing the pastry.

Roll out the third sheet of pastry to the same dimensions as the first two. Use a paring knife to cut 1-inch (2.5-cm) slits in the pastry in neat and overlapping rows. Gently pull apart the pastry over the assembled pastry and it should reveal little triangles. Place the third sheet of pastry over the second sheet covering the salmon, then use a sharp knife to cut away excess pastry, leaving a 1-inch (2.5-cm) border all around. Brush the entire pastry with the beaten egg.

Bake the salmon coulibiac for 45 to 50 minutes, until the pastry is a rich golden color.

Meanwhile, make the lemon sauce. Heat a small skillet over medium heat. Add the lemon juice, wine and shallot. Bring the liquids to a simmer and cook until the liquids are reduced to 2 tablespoons (30 ml), about 5 minutes. Add the butter, salt, dill and parsley and whisk until the butter is melted. Remove the sauce from the heat and pour it into a small ramekin for serving.

Remove the pastry from the oven and let it cool for at least 15 minutes prior to serving. To serve, use a long, serrated knife to slice the pastry into thick slices. Serve the salmon coulibiac with the lemon wedges and lemon sauce on the side.

FOR EGG WASH

1 large egg, beaten

LEMON SAUCE

2 tbsp (30 ml) lemon juice

¼ cup (60 ml) white wine

1 shallot, diced

3 tbsp (42 g) butter

Salt, as needed

Finely chopped fresh dill, as needed

Finely chopped fresh parsley, as needed

FOR SERVING

Lemon wedges, as needed

POTATO AND ONION PIEROGI

Вареники с Картошкой ✦ Vareniki s Kartoshkoy

These potato and caramelized onion pierogi, or dumplings, are the taste of my childhood. I remember making these in our little kitchen and my mom reminding me not to get filling on the edges of the dough. These pierogi are a little labor intensive, but they are well worth the effort. This recipe makes eighty dumplings; I usually prepare half of them fresh and freeze the rest for later.

YIELD: 80 PIEROGI

To make the dough, whisk the eggs, water and salt in a bowl until the mixture is smooth. Add 5 cups (625 g) of flour, 1 cup (125 g) at a time, stirring until a ball begins to form. Transfer the dough to a floured surface and knead it for 3 to 4 minutes, until it's smooth, firm and elastic. Wrap it in plastic wrap and chill in the refrigerator for at least 1 hour.

Meanwhile, place the potatoes in a large pot and cover them with water. Add the salt and bay leaves. Cook over medium-high heat for about 15 minutes, or until the potatoes are tender. Drain, then add ½ cup (112 g) of the butter and the cream. Mash the potatoes into a smooth puree, then add 2 tablespoons (4 g) of the dill and season with salt and black pepper.

Preheat a large skillet over medium heat and melt the remaining 2 tablespoons (28 g) of butter. Add the onions and sauté them for 10 to 12 minutes, until the onions are tender and lightly caramelized, but not burned. Remove from the heat; mix half with the potatoes and reserve half for serving.

Once the dough has rested, knead it again for 1 minute, then divide it into 4 pieces. Roll out 1 piece of dough on a floured work surface until it is about ⅛ inch (3 mm) thick, forming a large square or circle. Use a 1½-inch (4-cm) round cookie cutter to cut out circles, kneading unused portions and rolling out again until all the dough is used.

Place the remaining ½ cup (63 g) of flour in a small bowl and set it within reach. Flour your fingers, then place 2 tablespoons (30 g) of the filling into the middle of each dough circle. Pull the dough around the filling, pinching the edges to create a half-moon shape. Go over the seam twice to ensure a good seal, and avoid getting filling on the seams. Place the pierogi on a floured baking sheet in a single layer.

Bring a large pot of salted water to a boil over high heat and cook approximately 15 to 20 pierogi at a time; do not overcrowd the pot. Cook the fresh pierogi for 5 minutes, then remove with a slotted spoon and transfer to a large bowl. Serve with the caramelized onions, remaining dill and sour cream.

DOUGH

2 large eggs

1½ cups (360 ml) water

1 tsp salt

5½ cups (688 g) all-purpose flour, divided

FILLING

6 medium russet potatoes, peeled and cubed

2 tsp (10 g) salt, plus more as needed

2 dried bay leaves

½ cup (112 g) plus 2 tbsp (28 g) butter, divided

½ cup (120 ml) heavy cream

¼ cup (8 g) finely chopped fresh dill, divided

Ground black pepper, as needed

2 medium onions, diced

FOR SERVING

Sour cream, as needed

QUICK TIP: To freeze the pierogi, generously dust a large baking sheet with flour and place the shaped pierogi on the prepared baking sheet in a single layer. Freeze them overnight, then transfer them to an airtight container or freezer storage bag. They can be kept frozen for up to 6 months.

STUFFED BELL PEPPERS

Фаршированный Перец ✤ Farshirovoniy Perets

These bell peppers are packed with an incredible filling of beef, rice, onion and spices. This Slavic version includes dill and coriander and the peppers are braised in a sauce of tomato and sour cream. I love to pour the sauce over the peppers before serving to add extra moisture. I recommend using 85 percent lean ground beef, because the extra fat adds juiciness and flavor. This recipe would also work well with ground pork or a combination of pork, turkey or beef.

YIELD: 6 TO 7 SERVINGS

Preheat the oven to 375°F (191°C).

To make the stuffed bell peppers, preheat a large skillet over medium heat and add the butter. Allow the butter to melt, then add the onion, carrots and garlic. Sauté the vegetables over medium heat for 4 to 5 minutes, until the onion is translucent but not brown. Transfer all but ⅓ cup (80 g) of this mixture to a large bowl. Add the rice and stir to combine.

To make the sauce, add the broth, sour cream, ketchup and salt to the reserved vegetable mixture in the skillet. Whisk the mixture for 1 minute, then set the skillet aside.

Prepare the bell peppers for stuffing. Using a paring knife, cut around the stem and core, discarding the seeds and any white flesh. Place the bell peppers in a large roasting pan, baking dish or pot; the peppers should fit snugly.

Once the rice and onion mixture is cool enough to handle, add the beef, parsley, dill, salt, black pepper, paprika, garlic powder, cumin and coriander. With gloved hands, mix all the ingredients until they are uniform. Gently stuff each pepper generously with the filling.

Pour the sauce from the skillet over the bell peppers, then cover the roasting pan with a lid or foil. Bake the bell peppers for 1 hour, then uncover the roasting pan and bake for 10 minutes. Remove the bell peppers from the oven and use a large spoon to ladle the sauce from the bottom of the pan over the peppers. Allow the bell peppers to cool slightly before garnishing them with the dill and serving them with the sour cream on the side.

STUFFED BELL PEPPERS

2 tbsp (28 g) butter

1 large onion, diced

2 large carrots, grated

2 cloves garlic, minced

1 cup (185 g) cooked and cooled white or brown rice

6 to 7 large red, orange or yellow bell peppers

1 lb (450 g) 85% lean ground beef

1 tbsp (2 g) finely chopped fresh parsley

1 tbsp (2 g) finely chopped fresh dill

1 tbsp (15 g) salt

1 tsp ground black pepper

½ tsp paprika

½ tsp garlic powder

¼ tsp ground cumin

¼ tsp ground coriander

SAUCE

2 cups (480 ml) beef broth

2 tbsp (30 g) sour cream

2 tbsp (30 g) ketchup

½ tsp salt

FOR SERVING

Finely chopped fresh dill, as needed

Sour cream, as needed

BEEF AND GARLIC RICE PILAF

Плов ✣ Plov

This aromatic rice dish is one of the most-loved dishes across Eastern Europe, Asia and Russia! It's made with tender chunks of lamb or beef, loads of garlic and seasoned rice. Plov originated from Uzbekistan and Kazakhstan and is usually prepared outdoors in a large wok over open flames. Ukrainians and Russians have adopted this recipe and it's become a staple dish in their cuisines. My version of the recipe doesn't require an outdoor setup but is just as good! You can make this recipe even more quickly using a pressure cooker (see Quick Tip).

YIELD: 8 CUPS (1.9 KG)

Season the beef generously with salt as needed. Preheat a large sauté pan over high heat and add the oil. Working in batches so as to not overcrowd the pan, add the beef and sear it for 7 to 9 minutes, until it is well browned all over. Transfer the beef to a large bowl and set it aside.

Reduce the heat to medium. Add the onion, carrots and cloves of garlic to the sauté pan. Add more oil if needed to prevent sticking. Sauté the vegetables for 7 to 8 minutes, until the onion is tender and golden.

Return the beef to the pan and add the remaining 2 teaspoons (10 g) of salt, cumin, coriander, black pepper and paprika. Add the whole head of garlic and the beef broth, stir and increase the heat to high. Bring the broth to a boil. Cover the pan with a lid, reduce the heat to low and braise the beef for 1 to 1½ hours, or until it is tender.

Once the beef is braised, sprinkle the rice in an even layer over the beef. Make sure the rice is submerged under the liquid but do not stir it; the rice should remain on top of the beef.

Reduce the heat to low, cover the pan with a tight-fitting lid and cook for 20 to 25 minutes, until the rice is tender. Once the rice is cooked, let the pan stand, covered, for 5 minutes. Use a large fork to toss the rice with the beef and arrange the whole head of garlic on top. Sprinkle the pilaf with the parsley and serve it with the pickled cucumbers and pickled tomatoes on the side.

QUICK TIP: If you are using a pressure cooker, set the temperature to high or use the Meat setting. Reduce the beef broth to 2½ cups (600 ml) and cook the beef for approximately 20 minutes.

2½ to 3 lbs (1.1 to 1.4 kg) beef or lamb tri-tip, trimmed and cut into 1½-inch (4-cm) cubes

2 tsp (10 g) salt, plus more as needed, divided

2 tbsp (30 ml) grapeseed oil, plus more as needed

1 large onion, diced

3 large carrots, julienned

1 whole head plus 6 to 8 cloves garlic, divided

½ tsp ground cumin

½ tsp ground coriander

½ tsp ground black pepper

1 tsp smoked paprika

3 cups (720 ml) beef broth

1 cup (180 g) basmati or parboiled rice

2 tbsp (4 g) finely chopped fresh parsley

Pickled cucumbers and pickled tomatoes, as needed

STEWED BEEF AND POTATOES

Жаркое с Говядиной ✣ Zharkoye s Govyadenoy

This recipe brings back so many tasty memories! My dad used to make this dish for us on the weekends, sometimes with pork or chicken instead of beef. It's a simple, hearty recipe that's made with inexpensive ingredients and packed with incredible Eastern European flavor. Serve the potatoes with a side of pickles or try it with my Tomato and Cucumber Summer Salad (page 108).

YIELD: 6 SERVINGS

Preheat the oven to 350°F (177°C). Preheat a large Dutch oven over high heat. Add the oil and beef. Fry the beef for 6 to 7 minutes, until it is well browned all over, then transfer it to a medium bowl.

Reduce the heat to medium. Add the butter to the Dutch oven and allow it to melt. Add the onion, carrot, garlic and mushrooms. Sauté this mixture until the onion is translucent, 6 to 7 minutes. Return the beef to the Dutch oven and season the mixture with the salt, black pepper, cumin, coriander and smoked paprika. Add the flour and toss the ingredients together for 1 minute with a spatula, until they are well coated in the flour.

Add the wine and allow it to simmer for 1 minute, then add the broth and tomato sauce. Stir the mixture until the ingredients are well combined.

Stir the potatoes into the stew and sprinkle it with the parsley. Cover the Dutch oven with a lid and bake the stew for 1½ to 2 hours (the longer the baking time, the more tender the beef).

To serve, spoon the potatoes, beef and sauce into a bowl and sprinkle the stew with the dill.

QUICK TIP: *This recipe can be made using a slow cooker. Prepare the recipe as written, sautéing the beef, onion and carrots in a large skillet. Then place the beef, onion and carrots along with the remaining ingredients into the slow cooker and add only 1½ cups (360 ml) of broth. Cover the slow cooker and cook on high heat for 5 hours, or until the meat is very tender.*

1 tbsp (15 ml) grapeseed oil

1½ lbs (675 g) beef tri-tip, trimmed and cubed

2 tbsp (28 g) butter

1 large onion, diced

1 large carrot, grated

4 cloves garlic, minced

10 to 12 white mushrooms, thickly sliced

2 tsp (10 g) salt

1 tsp ground black pepper

1 tsp ground cumin

1 tsp ground coriander

1 tsp smoked paprika

2 tbsp (16 g) all-purpose flour

½ cup (120 ml) dry white wine

3 cups (720 ml) beef broth

1 cup (240 ml) tomato sauce

6 to 7 large russet potatoes, cubed

2 tbsp (4 g) finely chopped fresh parsley

Finely chopped fresh dill, as needed

BEEF STROGANOFF

Строганов ❖ Stroganov

This old-world Russian beef recipe has been around since the mid-nineteenth century. The original recipe was made with thin strips of sautéed beef dressed in sour cream. Since then, there have been many variations of the recipe, with the beef served over rice, potatoes or noodles. I pair my beef stroganoff with egg noodles and a combination of white wine and cream. The beef and sauce are also great over my Butter and Sour Cream Mashed Potatoes (page 94).

YIELD: 5 TO 6 SERVINGS

Preheat a large sauté pan over medium-high heat and add the oil. Season the beef generously with the salt and black pepper as needed. Working in batches so as not to overcrowd the pan, add the beef to the sauté pan and cook for 4 to 5 minutes, until it is well browned all over. Transfer the beef to a tray and cover to keep it warm.

Add the butter to the sauté pan and allow it to melt. Reduce the heat to medium. Add the onion and mushrooms and sauté until the mushrooms are golden, about 5 minutes. Add the garlic and cook for 1 minute. Add the wine, remaining 1½ teaspoons (8 g) salt, black pepper, paprika, dill and parsley. Cook the mixture for 1 to 2 minutes, until the wine has reduced.

Add the flour and toss the ingredients until they're well coated. Cook for 1 minute, then add half the milk and stir until the sauce has thickened, about 1 minute. Add the remaining milk, broth and cream. Bring the sauce to a simmer, reduce the heat to low and add the beef. Simmer for 4 to 5 minutes, stirring occasionally, until the sauce thickens some more.

To serve, pour the stroganoff sauce over the egg noodles and toss until they are well coated. Alternatively, serve the sauce and noodles separately, spooning the sauce over the noodles. Sprinkle the lemon juice (if using) over the noodles before serving.

2 tbsp (30 ml) canola or grapeseed oil

1½ lbs (675 g) beef tenderloin, thinly sliced

1½ tsp (8 g) salt, plus more as needed, divided

Ground black pepper, as needed

2 tbsp (28 g) butter

1 medium onion, diced

10 to 12 white mushrooms, thickly sliced

6 cloves garlic, minced

¼ cup (60 ml) white wine

1 tsp paprika

2 tbsp (4 g) finely chopped fresh dill

1 tbsp (2 g) finely chopped fresh parsley

¼ cup (31 g) all-purpose flour

1 cup (240 ml) whole milk

1 cup (240 ml) beef broth

½ cup (120 ml) heavy cream

6 oz (168 g) egg noodles, cooked

Fresh lemon juice, as needed (optional)

BEEF AND MUSHROOM CABBAGE ROLLS

Голубцы ✤ Golubtsi

Many countries have cabbage rolls, and Ukraine is no exception. This flavorful beef and mushroom version is bound to become a family favorite. The cabbage rolls are stuffed with beef, rice, mushrooms and onion, then cooked in a carrot-tomato sauce.

YIELD: ABOUT 30 ROLLS

Place the rice and water into a small saucepan over medium heat. Cover, bring to a simmer and then reduce the heat to low and cook about 20 minutes, or until the rice is tender. Fluff the rice with a fork and let it cool.

Meanwhile, use a sharp knife to cut around the hard core of the cabbage and discard it. Bring a large pot of water to a boil over high heat and add the cabbage. As the leaves soften, peel them away from the head using kitchen tongs and transfer them to a wire rack to cool. The leaves need to be translucent.

Preheat the oven to 375°F (191°C). Then heat a large skillet over medium heat and melt the butter. Add the onions, carrots, garlic and mushrooms. Sauté for 5 to 6 minutes, until the onions are translucent. Transfer two-thirds of the mixture to a large bowl, leaving the rest in the skillet.

To the onion-mushroom mixture in the skillet, add the tomato sauce, sour cream, sugar and broth. Season the mixture to taste with salt, black pepper and coriander. Bring to a simmer and cook for 3 to 4 minutes. Remove from the heat and pour about one-third of the sauce into the bottom of a large baking dish, oven-safe sauté pan or braising pot; reserve the rest for topping the rolls.

In a large bowl, combine the cooled rice, reserved onion-mushroom mixture, beef, egg, remaining 2 teaspoons (10 g) of salt, remaining 1 teaspoon of black pepper, remaining ½ teaspoon of coriander, cumin, paprika and garlic powder. Fold everything together until a uniform mixture forms.

To make the rolls, first trim off any hard pieces from the cabbage leaves and split the larger leaves in half. Use 2 to 3 tablespoons (30 to 45 g) of filling per roll, depending on what size you would like them to be. Place the filling on one edge of a cabbage leaf, then turn the leaf over the filling, rolling it and tucking any excess into the roll. Place the rolls in layers into the baking dish with the sauce. Pour the remaining tomato sauce over top. Cover with a lid or foil, then bake for 50 minutes. Remove the lid or foil and bake for 10 more minutes.

Allow the rolls to cool slightly, then sprinkle them with the dill and serve them with additional sour cream.

1 cup (180 g) white rice

1 extra-large green or napa cabbage

1 tbsp (14 g) butter

2 medium onions, diced

2 large carrots, grated

2 cloves garlic, minced

10 white mushrooms, diced

1 cup (240 ml) tomato sauce

¼ cup (60 g) sour cream, plus more as needed

½ tbsp (7 g) sugar

4 cups (960 ml) beef broth

2 tsp (10 g) salt, plus more as needed, divided

1 tsp ground black pepper, plus more as needed, divided

½ tsp ground coriander, plus more as needed, divided

1 lb (450 g) 85% lean ground beef

1 large egg

½ tsp ground cumin

½ tsp paprika

½ tsp garlic powder

Finely chopped fresh dill, as needed

QUICK TIPS: Make the cabbage rolls the night before and arrange them in a baking dish. Cover and refrigerate the dish until you are ready to bake.

For the slow cooker: Place the rolls and sauce into a slow cooker. Cover and cook on high for 6 to 7 hours, or until the beef is fully cooked.

SHISH KEBABS

Шашлычки ✣ Shashliki

No Slavic summer would be complete without Warm Fruit Compote (page 167), refreshing garden salads and some shish kebabs! Because shashliki are so popular, I'm including two recipes: a creamy marinade that works well for chicken or pork and a second recipe with wine and onion for beef and lamb.

Both recipes yield extra juicy and flavorful grilled meats that will not disappoint. I recommend marinating the meat overnight for best results. Serve the grilled meats with a side of baby potatoes and a salad, like my Tomato and Cucumber Summer Salad (page 108).

YIELD: 6 SERVINGS

CHICKEN OR PORK KEBABS

In a very large bowl, combine the onion, mayonnaise, sour cream, wine, cumin, coriander, paprika, garlic powder, black pepper, salt and dill. Whisk the ingredients together until a smooth sauce forms.

Cut the chicken or pork into 1½-inch (4-cm) chunks. Add the meat to the marinade and mix, making sure each piece is well coated. Cover the bowl and refrigerate overnight (or for at least 4 hours).

When you are ready to grill, preheat the outdoor gas grill to approximately 500°F (260°C). (For a more traditional cooking method, grill the meat over coals.) Thread the meat onto metal or wooden skewers and avoid overcrowding the meat on the skewers. If you are using wooden skewers, soak them in water for at least 30 minutes prior to threading the meat onto them.

Grill the kebabs for 18 to 20 minutes, rotating them every 5 or 6 minutes, until the meat's internal temperature reaches 165°F (74°C) for chicken or 145°F (63°C) for pork. Add the onion slices to the grill and cook them for about 10 minutes, turning them halfway through the cooking time.

Serve the kebabs with the grilled onion, a side of salad and potatoes and ketchup as a dipping sauce.

CHICKEN OR PORK

1 small onion, grated or pureed

¼ cup (55 g) mayonnaise

¼ cup (60 g) sour cream

¼ cup (60 ml) white wine

¼ tsp ground cumin

¼ tsp ground coriander

½ tsp paprika

1 tsp garlic powder

1 tsp ground black pepper

1 tbsp (15 g) salt

2 to 3 tbsp (4 to 6 g) finely chopped fresh dill

2½ to 3 lbs (1.1 to 1.4 kg) boneless, skinless chicken thigh or pork tenderloin

1 large onion, thickly sliced

BEEF OR LAMB KEBABS

In a very large bowl, whisk together the wine, onion, cilantro, garlic, salt, black pepper, paprika, cumin and coriander.

Trim the beef or lamb of any ligaments and hard fat and cut it into 1½-inch (4-cm) chunks. Add the meat to the marinade and toss to coat it evenly. Cover the bowl and marinate the meat for at least 8 hours (preferably overnight).

When you are ready to grill, preheat the outdoor gas grill to approximately 500°F (260°C). (For a more traditional cooking method, grill the meat over coals.) Thread the meat onto metal or wooden skewers and avoid overcrowding the meat on the skewers. If you are using wooden skewers, soak them in water for at least 30 minutes prior to threading the meat onto them.

Grill the kebabs for 15 to 18 minutes, rotating them every 5 or 6 minutes, until the internal temperature reaches 145°F (63°C). Add the onion slices to the grill and cook them for about 10 minutes, turning them halfway through the cooking time.

Serve the kebabs with the grilled onion, a side of salad and potatoes and ketchup as a dipping sauce.

*See photo on page 38.

QUICK TIP: In Ukraine and Russia, shashliki are prepared on a special coal grill called a **мангал** (mangal). It's a long, narrow iron box that's filled with coals and the shashliki are grilled over the open coals without any grill grates.

BEEF OR LAMB

1 cup (240 ml) dry red wine

1 large red onion, thinly sliced

¼ cup (8 g) finely chopped fresh cilantro or parsley

4 cloves garlic, minced

1 tbsp (15 g) salt

1 tsp ground black pepper

1 tsp paprika

½ tsp ground cumin

½ tsp ground coriander

2½ to 3 lbs (1.1 to 1.4 kg) boneless beef sirloin or leg of lamb

1 large onion, thickly sliced

CHICKEN KIEV

Курица по Киевски ✤ Kuritsa po Kievski

This buttery chicken dish was invented in the capital of Ukraine sometime in the 1800s. It was inspired by French cuisine, then it was adapted to include local ingredients available at that time. This dish is usually enjoyed with a side of potatoes and a light salad.

YIELD: 4 SERVINGS

To make the herbed butter, place the butter into a small glass bowl and heat it in the microwave until it has softened. Add the parsley, dill, salt, black pepper, garlic powder and paprika, stirring to create a uniform mixture. Transfer the butter to a sheet of plastic wrap. Gently roll it in the plastic wrap to create a sealed log shape. Place it into the refrigerator to set completely, about 1 hour.

Once the butter is cold and set, prepare the chicken. Preheat the oven to 425°F (218°C). Use a sharp knife to carefully cut a pocket into the side of each chicken breast, being careful not to cut all the way through. Lay the chicken breast open, cover it with a sheet of plastic wrap and use a meat mallet to pound the chicken breast until it is about ¼ inch (6 mm) thick. Season the chicken generously with the salt and black pepper.

Remove the butter from the refrigerator and cut the log into thin slices small enough to easily stuff the chicken. Stuff each chicken breast generously with the butter, then use toothpicks to gently secure the seams.

Pour the oil into a large, wide pot and heat it over medium-high heat until it reaches 275°F (135°C). Line a 9 x 13–inch (23 x 33–cm) glass baking dish with foil.

While the oil heats, set up a dredging station for the chicken. Arrange three shallow trays in a row: In the first, combine the flour, paprika and 1 teaspoon of salt; to the second, add the eggs; to the third, add the breadcrumbs. Coat each chicken breast in flour, then in the beaten eggs, then in the breadcrumbs.

Fry the chicken for 5 to 6 minutes per side, until it is golden brown, turning it gently with kitchen tongs. Remove the chicken from the oil and place into the baking dish. Bake the chicken breasts in the oven for 15 to 20 minutes, until the meat's internal temperature reaches 165°F (74°C).

Remove the chicken from the oven and let it rest for at least 5 minutes before carefully removing the toothpicks and thinly slicing the chicken. Don't cut the chicken until just before you serve it or all the hot butter will spill out too early.

HERBED BUTTER

1 cup (224 g) butter, cubed

¼ cup (8 g) finely chopped fresh parsley

¼ cup (8 g) finely chopped fresh dill

2 tsp (10 g) salt

½ tsp ground black pepper

1 tsp garlic powder

½ tsp paprika

CHICKEN

4 (5-oz [140-g]) boneless, skinless chicken breasts

1 tsp salt, plus more as needed

Ground black pepper, as needed

2 cups (480 ml) canola or grapeseed oil

1 cup (125 g) all-purpose flour

Paprika, as needed

2 large eggs, lightly beaten

1 cup (125 g) fine breadcrumbs

QUICK TIP: The herbed butter can be prepared a day before the chicken. Store it in the refrigerator until needed.

NAVY-STYLE PASTA WITH BEEF

Макароны По Флотски ✦ Makaroni po Flotski

The name of this pasta dish says it all: This navy-style pasta was originally served to maritime soldiers because it was so inexpensive to make. Since its creation, the general population of Eastern Europe has fallen in love with it. This simple dish uses stewed or ground meat, sautéed onion and the pasta of the cook's choice. (I like to make it with spaghetti.) It's a classic that you can come back to again and again. Try serving the pasta with grated cheese on top for extra flavor.

YIELD: 6 SERVINGS

- 1 lb (450 g) your favorite pasta
- 2 tbsp (28 g) butter, divided
- 1 lb (450 g) 85% lean ground beef
- 1 large onion, diced
- 4 to 5 cloves garlic, minced
- ¼ cup (60 g) ketchup or tomato paste
- 1 tsp salt
- Ground black pepper, as needed
- ½ tsp ground coriander
- ½ tsp paprika
- 1 cup (240 ml) beef broth
- 1 tbsp (2 g) finely chopped fresh parsley
- 1 tbsp (2 g) finely chopped fresh dill

Bring a large pot of salted water to a boil over high heat. Add the pasta and cook it according to the package's instructions. Drain the pasta but keep it covered and warm.

While the pasta is cooking, preheat a large skillet over medium-high heat and melt 1 tablespoon (14 g) of the butter. Add the beef and fry it for 7 to 9 minutes, breaking it into smaller pieces with a spatula or spoon, until it's well browned throughout.

Remove the beef from the skillet and set it aside. Add the remaining 1 tablespoon (14 g) of butter and the onion to the skillet. Sauté the onion for about 4 minutes, until it is tender, then add the garlic and cook for 1 minute.

Return the ground beef to the skillet and add the ketchup, salt, black pepper, coriander, paprika and broth. Stir the sauce until the ingredients are well combined, then reduce the heat to medium and simmer the mixture for about 5 minutes. Top it with the parsley and dill before serving.

BRAISED CABBAGE AND CHICKEN

Тушеная Капуста с Курицей ✦ Tushonaya Kapusta s Kuretsoy

Many Eastern European and Russian dishes were invented to utilize the meager ingredients that were available on hand, especially during the winter months. This braised cabbage dish is one of those recipes. My family's version of this dish has some extra additions, such as chicken thighs, mushrooms and bell peppers to add more protein, flavor and variety. It's a delicious and inexpensive dish that's good any time of year. Enjoy it with rustic rye bread or my Butter and Sour Cream Mashed Potatoes (page 94).

YIELD: 6 TO 8 SERVINGS

Grapeseed oil, as needed

1½ to 2 lbs (675 to 900 g) boneless, skinless chicken thighs, cubed

2½ tsp (10 g) salt, divided

½ tsp ground black pepper, divided

¼ cup (56 g) salted butter

3 large carrots, julienned

1 large red bell pepper, diced

10 white mushrooms, diced

1 medium sweet onion, diced

2 to 3 cloves garlic, minced

¼ tsp ground cumin

¼ tsp ground coriander

½ tsp smoked paprika

1 medium green cabbage, shredded

1 cup (150 g) sauerkraut

1 tbsp (2 g) finely chopped fresh dill

Preheat a large braising pan or cast-iron pan over medium-high heat and add a small amount of oil. Once the pan is hot, add the chicken thighs and season them with ½ teaspoon of salt and ¼ teaspoon of black pepper as needed. Fry the chicken for 5 to 6 minutes, until it is well browned all over. Transfer the chicken to a medium bowl and set it aside.

Reduce the heat to medium. Add the butter to the braising pan and allow the butter to melt. Add the carrots, bell pepper, mushrooms, onion and garlic. Sauté the vegetables for 5 to 7 minutes, until the onion is tender and translucent but not brown.

Return the chicken to the braising pan and season the mixture with the remaining 2 teaspoons (10 g) of salt, ¼ teaspoon of black pepper, cumin, coriander and paprika. Cook for 1 minute, then add the cabbage and sauerkraut. Using a large spatula, toss all the ingredients together.

Reduce the heat to medium-low. Cover the braising pan with a lid and cook the cabbage mixture for 20 minutes, stirring every 5 minutes. Serve the braised cabbage warm sprinkled with the dill and accompanied by a side of your choosing.

PORK MEATBALLS IN TOMATO SAUCE

Тефтели в Томатном Соусе ✤ Tefteli v Tomatnom Souce

This hearty and aromatic dish is perfect for dinner. The meatballs are made with juicy pork, sweet carrots, aromatic onion and vibrant dill, then cooked in a carrot-tomato sauce. This Eastern European version of tomato sauce is distinctly different than the Italian sauce most of us are accustomed to because it's sweeter and seasoned with dill. Serve these meatballs over my Butter and Sour Cream Mashed Potatoes (page 94) with pickles on the side for the ultimate Ukrainian experience!

YIELD: ABOUT 30 MEATBALLS

To make the sauce, preheat a large sauté pan over medium heat and add the butter. After the butter has melted, add the onion and carrots. Sauté this mixture for 5 to 6 minutes, until the carrot and onion are tender but not brown. Add the garlic during the last minute of cooking time. Transfer half the mixture to a large bowl, keeping the other half in the sauté pan.

To the sauté pan, add the tomato sauce, broth, salt, black pepper, smoked paprika, coriander and cumin. Stir the ingredients together and set the sauce aside.

To make the meatballs, add the pork, egg, mayonnaise, breadcrumbs, salt, black pepper, paprika, coriander and cumin to the carrot and onion mixture in the large bowl. Gently fold everything together for 1 minute, being careful not to overmix. Using a 1½-tablespoon (23-g) scoop, measure out the meat for each meatball, then roll it into a ball and place onto a large tray.

Preheat a large skillet over medium heat and add 1 tablespoon (15 ml) of oil. Fry the meatballs in small batches to avoid overcrowding the skillet. Fry for 2 minutes on each side, turning the meatballs when they're browned, about 5 to 6 minutes total of cooking time. (The meatballs do not need to be completely cooked, just browned). Add more oil as needed between batches of meatballs.

Gently place the meatballs into the prepared sauce without stirring. Cover the sauté pan and bring the sauce to a simmer over medium heat. Reduce the heat to low and cook the meatballs, covered, for 45 minutes, stirring and turning them occasionally with a wooden spoon.

Once the meatballs are done, sprinkle them with the dill and parsley and serve them with the Butter and Sour Cream Mashed Potatoes and pickles on the side.

SAUCE

2 tbsp (28 g) butter

1 large onion, diced

4 medium carrots, grated

3 cloves garlic, minced

1½ cups (360 ml) tomato sauce

1½ cups (360 ml) vegetable or chicken broth

1 tsp salt

½ tsp ground black pepper

½ tsp smoked paprika

¼ tsp ground coriander

¼ tsp ground cumin

MEATBALLS

1 lb (450 g) ground pork

1 large egg

¼ cup (55 g) mayonnaise

½ cup (63 g) finely ground breadcrumbs

1 tsp salt

¼ tsp ground black pepper

½ tsp paprika

½ tsp ground coriander

½ tsp ground cumin

Canola or grapeseed oil, as needed

2 tbsp (4 g) finely chopped fresh dill

1 tbsp (2 g) finely chopped fresh parsley

FOR SERVING

1 batch Butter and Sour Cream Mashed Potatoes (page 94)

Pickles, as needed

CHICKEN CUTLETS WITH GRAVY

Котлеты с Подливой ✣ Kotleti s Podlivoy

This warming and hearty dish is a prime example of a traditional Eastern European dinner: juicy chicken cutlets served over a bed of creamy potatoes and gravy. This recipe is a combination of several of my recipes, including the Carrot and Mushroom Gravy (page 97) and Butter and Sour Cream Mashed Potatoes (page 94) and is the type of dish I grew up enjoying often. It's inexpensive and easy to put together and goes great with a side of pickles.

YIELD: 5 TO 6 SERVINGS

Place the chicken, egg, onion, salt, black pepper, coriander, breadcrumbs, parsley and dill into a large bowl. Using your hands or a spatula, combine the ingredients just until they are well mixed.

Use a 2-tablespoon (30-g) measuring scoop to measure out the meat mixture for each cutlet. Roll the meat into a ball, then pat the ball into a small disk and place it onto a tray.

Preheat a large skillet over medium heat and add the oil. Once the oil is hot, add the cutlets and reduce the heat to medium-low. (If needed, fry the cutlets in two batches, adding more oil as needed.) Fry the cutlets for 4 to 5 minutes per side, until they are golden and their internal temperature reaches 165°F (74°C). Remove the cutlets from the skillet and cover to keep them warm.

To serve, ladle the Carrot and Mushroom Gravy over a bed of the Butter and Sour Cream Mashed Potatoes and top the potatoes with the cutlets. Serve the cutlets with the pickles on the side.

QUICK TIP: *This dish can also be enjoyed with my Juicy Beef Cutlets (page 29) instead of chicken. You can serve the cutlets and gravy with pasta or egg noodles as well.*

1 lb (450 g) ground chicken or turkey

1 large egg

1 medium onion, grated

2 tsp (10 g) salt

½ tsp ground black pepper

½ tsp ground coriander

½ cup (55 g) plain breadcrumbs

1 tbsp (2 g) finely chopped fresh parsley

1 tbsp (2 g) finely chopped fresh dill

2 tbsp (30 ml) canola or grapeseed oil, plus more as needed

1 batch Carrot and Mushroom Gravy (page 97)

1 batch Butter and Sour Cream Mashed Potatoes (page 94)

Pickles, as needed

POTATO LATKES WITH CHICKEN

Картопляники с Мясом ✦ Kartoplyaniki s Myasom

These Ukrainian potato latkes are latkes like you've never had before. The potato pancakes are first fried, then served with a chicken, garlic and onion sauce. The results? Soft, delicate and garlicky latkes that are perfect with sour cream. My mom would make these Ukrainian latkes at least once a month, even though they do take a bit of time to prepare. Now, I can't have them any other way!

YIELD: ABOUT 25 PANCAKES

To make the latkes, grate the potatoes into a very large bowl. Cover the potatoes in ice-cold water and let them soak for 5 minutes, then drain them. Repeat this process 3 times to rid the potatoes of their starch.

Add the onions, garlic, sour cream, eggs, flour, salt and black pepper to the potatoes. Use a large spatula to fold the ingredients together until a uniform batter forms. If the batter is too runny, add an additional ¼ cup (31 g) flour.

Preheat a large skillet over low heat and add the oil. Use a 2-tablespoon (30-g) scoop to transfer the potato batter to the skillet. Flatten the latkes slightly into a pancake shape, then cook them for about 5 minutes per side, until they are golden brown and the potatoes are cooked. Transfer the cooked latkes to a large baking dish. Cover the baking dish with foil to keep the latkes warm and repeat this process with the remaining batter, adding more oil to the skillet as needed.

To make the sauce, preheat a large skillet over medium heat and add the oil. Once the oil is hot, add the chicken and season it with salt and black pepper. Fry the chicken for about 5 minutes, then add the onion. Cook until the chicken is golden brown and cooked through, 4 to 5 minutes. Add the garlic and fry for about 30 seconds, then add the water. Bring the sauce to a simmer and cook for 1 minute.

Pour the chicken sauce over the latkes arranged in the baking dish and garnish the latkes with the dill. Serve the latkes with the sour cream and pickles on the side.

QUICK TIP: For a truly unique, old-world dish, follow the recipe as written and add this additional step: Preheat the oven to 400°F (204°C). Add an additional ⅓ cup (80 ml) water to the latkes and sauce in the baking dish. Cover the baking dish with foil and bake the latkes for 30 minutes. Garnish them with the dill and serve with sour cream and pickles on the side.

LATKES

5 lbs (2.3 kg) russet potatoes, peeled

2 medium onions, grated

4 cloves garlic, pressed

¼ cup (60 g) sour cream

4 large eggs

1½ cups (188 g) all-purpose flour, plus more as needed

1 tbsp (15 g) salt

2 tsp (4 g) ground black pepper

1 tbsp (15 ml) canola or grapeseed oil, plus more as needed

SAUCE

2 tbsp (30 ml) grapeseed oil

1 lb (450 g) boneless, skinless chicken thighs, cubed

1 tsp salt

Ground black pepper, as needed

1 small onion, diced

6 to 7 cloves garlic, minced

⅓ cup (80 ml) water

FOR SERVING

Finely chopped fresh dill, as needed

Sour cream, as needed

Pickles, as needed

WARMING SOUPS AND EASY SIDE DISHES

Soups are an integral part of Eastern European cuisine—they're hearty, filling and inexpensive to make. Plus, they keep you warm during those long winter days! This chapter has all my favorite Eastern European soups, as well as several traditional side dishes. In this section, you'll find warming soups that can be enjoyed year-round, like my favorites, Classic Beef Borscht (page 77) and Chicken Buckwheat Soup (page 90). There's even a cold, refreshing cucumber soup recipe on page 86 that's perfect for summer. Also included in this chapter are traditional and everyday side dishes like Dill and Garlic Potatoes (page 93) and Mushroom Buckwheat (page 98). These side recipes go very well with the hearty meat dishes from the previous chapter.

CLASSIC BEEF BORSCHT

Борщ ✤ Borshch

If I had to pick one recipe that captured the spirit of Ukrainian and Russian cuisine, borscht would be my first choice! It's probably the one dish that most everyone has at least heard of, if not tried. There are many versions of classic red borscht. Even my parents have different recipes—my dad makes his with beans! My recipe with beef is very aromatic, flavorful and on the thicker side with loads of veggies and beet greens. This recipe is great to make on the weekend and enjoy during the week, because borscht is one of those dishes that tastes better after it stands in the fridge overnight and develops more flavor.

YIELD: 14 CUPS (3.4 L)

Preheat a large pot over medium-high heat and add the oil and butter. Once the butter has melted, add the beef, season it with salt and increase the heat to high. Cook the meat until it is well browned all over, 7 to 8 minutes.

Add the onion, carrots and celery and toss to combine. Reduce the heat to medium and cook the mixture for 4 to 5 minutes, until the onion is translucent. Add the garlic, then season the mixture with more salt and the black pepper, cumin, coriander and sugar. Add the beets, broth, water and tomato sauce. Cover the pot with a lid and bring the mixture to a simmer. Reduce the heat to low and cook the soup for 45 minutes, covered, until the beef is tender.

Once the beef is tender, add the potatoes and cook the soup for 10 minutes. Add the beet greens, lemon juice, dill and parsley and cook for 5 minutes. Remove the soup from the heat, cover the pot and let the soup stand for 15 minutes before serving with a dollop of the sour cream and the bread.

QUICK TIP: To cut down on cooking time, use a pressure cooker for the beef. Prepare the recipe as written through adding the water, then cook the beef and vegetables in a pressure cooker under high pressure for 12 to 15 minutes (or use the preprogrammed Meat setting). Proceed with the recipe as written.

1 tbsp (15 ml) grapeseed oil

2 tbsp (28 g) butter

1½ lbs (675 g) beef tri-tip, trimmed and cubed

Salt, as needed

1 large onion, diced

3 medium carrots, diced

2 large ribs celery, diced

2 cloves garlic, minced

Ground black pepper, as needed

½ tsp ground cumin

½ tsp ground coriander

½ tbsp (7 g) sugar

3 medium beets, diced

4 cups (960 ml) beef broth

4 cups (960 ml) water

1 cup (240 ml) tomato sauce

4 to 5 medium russet potatoes, peeled and cubed

3 to 4 cups (400 to 500 g) finely chopped beet greens or thinly sliced cabbage

1 tbsp (15 ml) fresh or bottled lemon juice

2 tbsp (4 g) finely chopped fresh dill

2 tbsp (4 g) finely chopped fresh parsley

Sour cream, as needed

Rustic bread, as needed

SORREL AND CHICKEN GREEN BORSCHT

Зеленый Борщ ✤ Zeloniy Borshch

This green borscht is made with chicken, eggs and the sour sorrel herb. Sorrel is usually added to recipes in small quantities in other cuisines, but in Eastern Europe and Ukraine, it's used by the bundles! Sorrel is a seasonal summer herb, so this soup is enjoyed almost exclusively in the summertime. Serve this borscht with rustic bread and with a bit of sour cream for a creamy version.

Sorrel can be found in some stores right next to other fresh herbs, such as basil and dill. Because this soup calls for a large quantity, I recommend visiting your local Russian market to find large bundles. You can purchase an extra bundle or two, chop them and freeze them to use when fresh sorrel is not readily available.

YIELD: 12 CUPS (2.9 L)

Preheat a large skillet over medium heat and add the butter. Once the butter has melted, add the chicken and fry it for 5 to 6 minutes, until it is well browned all over. Transfer the chicken to a large pot.

In the same skillet, combine the onion, carrots and celery. Sauté this mixture for 4 to 5 minutes, until the onion is translucent but not brown. Add the vegetables to the pot. Add the broth, water, salt, black pepper and garlic powder. Bring the soup to a boil over high heat.

Add the potatoes and reduce the heat to medium. Cook the soup for 15 minutes, until the potatoes are tender.

Once the potatoes are cooked, add the eggs, sorrel, parsley and dill. Cook the soup for 1 minute, then remove it from the heat. Allow the soup to stand for 20 to 30 minutes, then serve it with the bread and sour cream on the side, if you'd like.

1 tbsp (14 g) butter or 1 tbsp (15 ml) grapeseed oil

1 lb (450 g) boneless, skinless chicken thighs, cubed

1 medium onion, diced

2 large carrots, diced

1 large rib celery, diced

6 cups (1.4 L) chicken broth

6 cups (1.4 L) water

2 tsp (10 g) salt

1 tsp ground black pepper

1 tsp garlic powder

4 to 5 medium russet potatoes, peeled and cubed

6 large hard-boiled eggs, diced

2 large bunches fresh sorrel, finely chopped

⅓ cup (11 g) finely chopped fresh parsley

2 tbsp (2 g) finely chopped fresh dill

Rustic bread, as needed (optional)

¼ cup (60 g) sour cream (optional)

FISH BROTH SOUP

Уха ✤ Uha

If you love seafood, you're going to love this tasty and warming fish broth soup! Since fishing is such an important part of Eastern European culture, seafood dishes like this simple soup are plentiful. My dad and brothers are avid fishermen and, as my siblings and I were growing up, we enjoyed this soup often. It's an easy recipe that can be made with just about any fish: salmon, arctic char (see photo), trout, sturgeon, bass or snapper. For this recipe to work well, it's important to use the full fish, including the bones and head.

YIELD: 12 CUPS (2.8 L)

To make the broth, clean the fish of any insides and rinse it well. Next, use a sharp knife to fillet the fish: Starting at the head, make a cut around the head, then slide the knife along the spine, making a smooth cut to the tail. Repeat this process on the other side. If desired, skin the fillets: Lay the fish fillets skin-side down, lay the knife flat and carefully cut away the skin. Cut the fish into 1-inch (2.5-cm) cubes, then transfer the cubes to a large bowl and place the bowl in the refrigerator.

Cut the head from the remaining fish carcass, then use kitchen shears to carefully clip away the gills and discard them. (This step is very important—the broth will taste bitter if cooked with the gills.)

Place the whole fish carcass (head, tail and bones) into a large pot and add the water. Add the onion, garlic, carrots, celery, salt, peppercorns, bay leaves, coriander and cumin. Bring the broth to a simmer over high heat, then reduce the heat to low and cook for 45 minutes.

Strain the broth several times using a fine-mesh strainer lined with cheesecloth; discard the fish bones, fish head, vegetables, peppercorns and bay leaves.

To make the soup, pour the strained broth into a clean large pot over high heat. Add the potatoes, carrots and onion. Bring the soup to a simmer, then reduce the heat to medium and cook for about 10 minutes. Remove the fish from the refrigerator, add it to the soup and cook for 5 minutes. (Be sure not to overcook the fish. It will continue to cook in the hot broth.) Remove the soup from the heat and add the dill and parsley. Sprinkle the green onions on the soup (if using) and serve it with the bread on the side (if using).

BROTH

1 (2- to 3-lb [900-g to 1.4-kg]) whole fish, including head

12 cups (2.8 L) water

1 medium onion, coarsely chopped

4 cloves garlic

2 large carrots, coarsely chopped

2 ribs celery, coarsely chopped

1 tbsp (15 g) salt

10 to 12 black peppercorns

3 to 4 dried bay leaves

½ tsp ground coriander

½ tsp ground cumin

SOUP

3 large russet potatoes, cubed

2 to 3 large carrots, thinly sliced

1 medium onion, diced

1 tbsp (2 g) finely chopped fresh dill

1 tbsp (2 g) finely chopped fresh parsley

Finely chopped green onions, as needed (optional)

Rustic bread, as needed (optional)

CHICKEN MEATBALL SOUP

Суп с Фрикадельками ❖ Soup s Frikadel'kami

I have so many warm memories associated with this soup! It reminds me of cold and snowy winter evenings and the aroma of something delicious cooking in the kitchen. It's a warm and uplifting soup with the most delicious chicken meatballs. But don't wait until winter to try it—it's great year-round. The meatballs are seasoned with fresh dill and parsley, which give the soup incredible flavor. Enjoy it with a baguette smeared with sour cream on the side.

YIELD: 12 CUPS (2.9 L)

To make the soup, preheat a large pot over medium heat and add a small amount of oil. Add the celery, carrots and onion and sauté this mixture for 6 to 8 minutes, until the onion is tender but not brown. Add the garlic and cook for 1 minute.

Add the broth, water, bay leaves, salt, black pepper and paprika and stir. Increase the heat to high and bring the soup to a simmer. Reduce the heat to medium and simmer for 15 to 30 minutes.

Meanwhile, make the meatballs. In a large bowl, combine the chicken, onion, egg, salt, black pepper, parsley, dill and breadcrumbs. Use a spatula to mix all the ingredients together for about 1 minute, just until well combined.

Use a 1-tablespoon (15-g) measuring spoon to scoop out the meat mixture for each meatball. Scoop the mixture into your hand, then gently roll the meat into a ball and set it on a tray. Once all the meatballs have been shaped, set the tray of meatballs aside.

Add the potatoes to the soup and cook them for 7 to 8 minutes. Gently drop the meatballs into the soup and do not stir. Continue cooking the soup for 7 to 8 minutes, just until the meatballs and potatoes are cooked. The meatballs will float to the surface as they cook. Remove the soup from the heat and add the parsley and dill. Discard the bay leaves before serving.

SOUP

Canola or grapeseed oil, as needed

2 large ribs celery, diced

2 large carrots, diced

1 large onion, diced

4 cloves garlic, minced

6 cups (1.4 L) chicken broth

6 cups (1.4 L) water

2 dried bay leaves

1 tbsp (15 g) salt

1 tsp ground black pepper

1 tsp paprika

4 to 5 large russet potatoes, peeled and cubed

1 tbsp (2 g) finely chopped fresh parsley

1 tbsp (2 g) finely chopped fresh dill

MEATBALLS

1 lb (450 g) ground chicken or turkey

1 small onion, grated

1 large egg

1 tsp salt

½ tsp ground black pepper

1 tbsp (2 g) finely chopped fresh parsley

1 tbsp (2 g) finely chopped fresh dill

¼ cup (31 g) finely ground breadcrumbs

SWEET AND SOUR BEEF SOUP

Солянка ✤ Solyanka

This traditional Russian soup is known as the "hangover cure" because of its briny flavor, which is thanks to the pickles, olives and capers. This sweet and sour soup has a tomato-based broth and is made with three different types of meat: beef, sausage and bacon. Talk about delicious! If you enjoy my Classic Beef Borscht (page 77), you'll love this recipe.

YIELD: 14 CUPS (3.4 L)

Heat a large pot over medium heat. Add the bacon. Render the bacon until it's golden and crispy, 4 to 5 minutes. Remove the bacon from the pot with a slotted spoon and place it in a large bowl.

Add the sausage to the pot and fry it for 3 to 4 minutes, until it is caramelized. Transfer the sausage to the bowl with the bacon. Add the beef to the pot and season it generously as needed with salt and black pepper. Add 1 tablespoon (15 ml) of the oil to prevent the beef from sticking, if necessary. Sauté the beef for 6 to 8 minutes, until it is well browned all over. Remove the beef and add it to the sausage and bacon.

Add the onion, celery and carrots to the pot. Add the remaining 1 tablespoon (15 ml) of oil to prevent the vegetables from sticking, if necessary. Sauté this mixture for 4 to 5 minutes, then add the garlic and cook for 1 minute, or until the onion is tender and translucent. Return the beef, sausage and bacon to the pot.

Add the water, broth, tomatoes, tomato paste, the remaining 1 tablespoon (15 g) of salt, 1 teaspoon black pepper, sugar, paprika and coriander. Stir to combine and increase the heat to high. Cover the pot and allow the soup to come to a boil. Reduce the heat to low and simmer the soup for 30 to 45 minutes, or until the beef is tender. (Some cuts might require longer cooking times.)

Add the pickles, olives, capers, parsley and dill and cook for 2 to 3 minutes, then remove the soup from the heat. Allow the soup to stand for 30 minutes. Serve the soup with a lemon slice in each bowl.

6 slices thick-cut bacon, diced

1 (12-oz [336-g]) kielbasa sausage, thinly sliced

1 lb (450 g) beef roast or tri-tip, cubed

1 tbsp (15 g) salt, plus more as needed, divided

1 tsp ground black pepper, plus more as needed, divided

2 tbsp (30 ml) grapeseed oil, divided (optional)

1 medium onion, diced

2 large ribs celery, diced

2 to 3 large carrots, diced

3 to 4 cloves garlic, minced

4 cups (960 ml) water

4 cups (960 ml) beef broth

1 (14-oz [392-g]) can petite diced tomatoes, undrained

½ cup (120 g) tomato paste

1 tbsp (13 g) sugar

1 tsp paprika

½ tsp coriander

6 to 8 medium kosher dill pickles, diced

1 cup (125 g) black or green olives, thickly sliced

1 tbsp (9 g) capers

2 tbsp (4 g) finely chopped fresh parsley

2 tbsp (4 g) finely chopped fresh dill

Lemon slices, as needed

COLD CUCUMBER SUMMER SOUP

Окрошка ✤ Okroshka

There's nothing more refreshing in the hot summer months than Russian okroshka! This cold cucumber soup is made with a tart and creamy broth, diced ham and eggs, radishes and, of course, cucumbers. I make my soup with buttermilk (you can also use a combination of sour cream and kvass). The slightly tart broth is the perfect complement to the crunchy vegetables and salty ham pieces. This soup can be made with or without the diced cooked potatoes; they can be omitted to cut down on prep time.

YIELD: 14 CUPS (3.4 L)

Bring a large pot of salted water to a boil over high heat and add the potatoes and eggs. Cook the eggs for 10 minutes, then remove them with a slotted spoon and place them into an ice bath to cool. Cook the potatoes until they are fork-tender, an additional 10 to 15 minutes, then remove them from the pot to cool. Once the potatoes and eggs are cool enough to handle, peel and dice them into pea-sized pieces.

In a separate large pot, whisk together the buttermilk, broth, salt, dill, parsley and black pepper.

Add the potatoes, eggs, ham, radishes, cucumbers and green onions and stir to combine. Transfer the soup to the refrigerator. Serve the soup chilled.

3 medium waxy potatoes

4 large eggs

4 cups (960 ml) cultured buttermilk

4 cups (960 ml) vegetable broth

1 tsp salt

2 tbsp (4 g) finely chopped fresh dill

1 tbsp (2 g) finely chopped fresh parsley

Ground black pepper, as needed

1½ cups (225 g) diced ham or cooked chicken breast

10 to 12 large radishes, diced

4 medium cucumbers, diced

3 green onions, diced

SPLIT PEA AND HAM SOUP

Гороховый Суп ✤ Gorohoviy Soup

My sister Nina's recipe for split pea soup is simple and delicious. Whenever she makes this amazing soup for our family, it's gone in no time! It's an inexpensive Ukrainian comfort food that's especially nice when you're feeling under the weather. Make sure to soak the split peas overnight to cut down the cooking time.

YIELD: 14 CUPS (3.4 L)

Place the split peas in a large bowl and cover them with enough water that they are submerged by at least 2 inches (5 cm). Cover the bowl and let the peas soak overnight. The next day, rinse the peas thoroughly with cold water and drain them.

In a large pot over high heat, combine the broth, water, split peas, salt, black pepper, garlic powder, coriander, cumin, oregano and basil. Bring the soup to a boil. Reduce the heat to medium and cook the soup for about 15 minutes.

Meanwhile, preheat a large skillet over medium heat. Add the sausage and sauté for 3 to 4 minutes, until it has browned. Add the butter, carrots, onion and celery and sauté for 3 to 4 minutes, until the onion is translucent.

Add the sausage and onion mixture, parsley and lemon juice to the soup. Cook the soup for an additional 15 minutes, until the peas are completely cooked.

QUICK TIP: If you prefer a thinner soup, use 6 cups (1.4 L) of water.

2 cups (450 g) dried green split peas

4 cups (960 ml) chicken or beef broth

4 cups (960 ml) water (see Quick Tip)

2 tsp (10 g) salt

Ground black pepper, as needed

1 tsp garlic powder

½ tsp ground coriander

½ tsp ground cumin

½ tsp dried oregano

½ tsp dried basil

1 (12-oz [336-g]) smoked kielbasa sausage, diced

1 tbsp (14 g) butter

2 medium carrots, diced

1 large onion, diced

2 large ribs celery, diced

1 large bunch fresh parsley, finely chopped

1 tbsp (15 ml) fresh lemon juice

CHICKEN BUCKWHEAT SOUP

Куриный Суп с Гречкой ❖ Kuriniy Soup s Grechkoy

Buckwheat is equivalent to rice in Eastern European cuisine and is used in many dishes, sweet and savory alike. It's a hearty and delicious grain-like seed that's versatile and perfect for soups like this one. This aromatic and easy soup recipe is especially great in fall and winter.

YIELD: 14 CUPS (3.4 L)

In a large pot over medium heat, combine the broth and water. Let the liquid warm while you move on to the next step.

Preheat a large skillet over medium heat and add a small amount of oil. Add the chicken, season it with salt as needed and fry it for 5 to 6 minutes, until it is well browned all over. Transfer the chicken to the pot.

To the same skillet, add the mushrooms and more oil to prevent sticking, if necessary. Sauté the mushrooms for 6 to 7 minutes, until they are well browned. Season the mushrooms lightly with salt and transfer them to the pot.

In the same skillet, combine the onion, carrots and celery. Sauté the mixture for about 5 minutes, until the onion is translucent. Add the garlic and sauté for 1 minute. Transfer the mixture to the pot.

Season the soup with the remaining 2 teaspoons (10 g) of salt, black pepper, coriander and smoked paprika. Cover the pot, increase the heat to medium-high and bring the soup to a boil. Reduce the heat to medium-low and simmer the soup for 10 minutes, then add the buckwheat. Continue cooking the soup over medium-low heat for 20 minutes, until the buckwheat is tender. Season the soup with the parsley and dill and serve.

6 cups (1.4 L) chicken broth

6 cups (1.4 L) water

Grapeseed oil, as needed

1 to 1½ lbs (450 to 675 g) boneless, skinless chicken breasts or thighs, cubed

2 tsp (10 g) salt, plus more as needed, divided

10 to 12 white mushrooms, thinly sliced

1 large onion, diced

2 medium carrots, diced

2 large ribs celery, diced

4 cloves garlic, minced

½ tsp ground black pepper

½ tsp ground coriander

½ tsp smoked paprika

1 cup (170 g) buckwheat

2 tbsp (4 g) finely chopped fresh parsley

2 tbsp (4 g) finely chopped fresh dill

DILL AND GARLIC POTATOES

Тушеная Картошка ✥ Tushonaya Kartoshka

This easy, versatile and flavor-packed recipe is the perfect complement to grilled or braised meats. The potatoes are simply cut into large chunks, then dressed with butter, dill and pressed fresh garlic. Personally, I love to use baby potatoes for this dish, because they're sweet and delicious. These are garlicky, herby potatoes that are anything but boring!

YIELD: 12 CUPS (3.9 KG)

3 lbs (1.4 kg) russet or baby potatoes
1 tbsp (15 g) salt, plus more as needed
3 to 4 dried bay leaves
1 small onion, diced
⅓ cup (75 g) salted butter, melted
8 to 10 cloves garlic, pressed
½ cup (16 g) finely chopped fresh dill
¼ cup (8 g) finely chopped fresh parsley
2 to 3 green onions, diced
Ground black pepper, as needed

If you are using russet potatoes, peel the potatoes and cut them into 1½-inch (4-cm) cubes. If you are using baby potatoes, leave them unpeeled and whole. Place the potatoes in a large pot and cover them completely with water. Add the salt, bay leaves and onion to the water.

Bring the water to a boil over high heat and cook the potatoes for 14 to 15 minutes, just until they are tender. (Do not overcook the potatoes, otherwise they will lose their shape.) Drain the potatoes and discard the bay leaves. If you are using baby potatoes, cut the larger ones in half. Transfer the potatoes to a large bowl.

Pour the butter over the potatoes, then add the garlic, dill, parsley, green onions, black pepper and additional salt to taste. Use a large spoon to gently toss the potatoes until they're well coated in the butter and dill.

BUTTER AND SOUR CREAM MASHED POTATOES

Картошка Пюре ✤ Kartoshka Puree

My mom makes the best mashed potatoes, and this is the recipe she always uses, which was passed down from her mother. These mashed potatoes are made with sweet onion and loads of butter and sour cream. Use full-fat sour cream for rich, creamy potatoes that make an ideal base for braised meats and vegetables, cutlets and even grilled kebabs.

YIELD: 10 CUPS (3.3 KG)

Place the potatoes, onion, peppercorns, bay leaves and salt into a large pot. Fill the pot with enough water to cover the potatoes completely.

Bring the potatoes to a boil over high heat, then reduce the heat to medium. Cook the potatoes for 16 to 18 minutes, or until they are fork-tender. Discard the peppercorns and bay leaves. Carefully drain the water.

Cut the butter into small chunks and add it to the hot potatoes. Allow the butter to melt for 2 to 3 minutes, then add the sour cream and use a potato masher to puree the potatoes. Season the potatoes with additional salt, if necessary and garnish with fresh dill (if using).

5 lbs (2.3 kg) russet potatoes, peeled and cut into large cubes

1 small sweet onion, diced

10 black peppercorns

3 to 4 dried bay leaves

2 tbsp (30 g) salt, plus more as needed

1 cup (224 g) salted butter

¼ cup (60 g) sour cream

1 tbsp (2 g) finely chopped fresh dill, for garnish (optional)

CARROT AND MUSHROOM GRAVY

Подлива с Грибами ❧ Podliva s Gribami

This is the gravy of Eastern Europe. This creamy and chunky gravy can be enjoyed with pasta, noodles, mashed potatoes and a variety of meats and cutlets. It's made with carrots, mushrooms, onion, garlic and sour cream. I also add dill and parsley to really highlight the Eastern European flavors. I use this recipe for my Chicken Cutlets with Gravy (page 71) and serve it with my Butter and Sour Cream Mashed Potatoes (page 94).

YIELD: 4 CUPS (960 ML)

Preheat a large sauté pan over medium-high heat and add the butter. Once the butter has melted, add the mushrooms. Sauté the mushrooms for 5 to 7 minutes, until they are golden and tender. Add the onion, carrot and garlic. Reduce the heat to medium and cook for about 5 minutes, stirring often, until the onion is tender.

Season the mixture with the salt, black pepper, smoked paprika and coriander. Add the flour and toss until all the ingredients are coated. Cook for 1 minute.

Whisk in the broth and cook for 2 to 3 minutes, until the mixture thickens. Add the milk and sour cream. Whisk the mixture for about 1 minute, until it is uniform.

Add the parsley and dill and reduce the heat to medium-low. Simmer the gravy for 3 to 4 minutes, until it is thick, stirring often. Remove the gravy from the heat and keep it covered until you are ready to serve.

¼ cup (56 g) butter

10 white mushrooms, thickly sliced

1 small onion, diced

1 large carrot, grated

3 to 4 cloves garlic, minced

1 tsp salt

Ground black pepper, as needed

½ tsp smoked paprika

¼ tsp ground coriander

¼ cup (31 g) all-purpose flour

1½ cups (360 ml) chicken broth

1½ cups (360 ml) milk

¼ cup (60 g) sour cream

1 tbsp (2 g) finely chopped fresh parsley

1 tbsp (2 g) finely chopped fresh dill

MUSHROOM BUCKWHEAT

Гречка с Грибами ✤ Grechka s Gribami

This simple and delicious buckwheat side dish is great in place of pasta or mashed potatoes. The buckwheat for this aromatic recipe is cooked in broth and combined with sautéed mushrooms. Make sure to cook the buckwheat according to package instructions—otherwise, it will turn into mush.

YIELD: 4 TO 6 SERVINGS

2 tbsp (28 g) butter

10 to 12 white mushrooms, thickly sliced

1 medium onion, diced

2 cups (480 ml) chicken broth

1 cup (170 g) buckwheat

2 tsp (10 g) salt

½ tsp ground black pepper

¼ tsp ground coriander

¼ tsp paprika

Preheat a large skillet over medium heat and add the butter. Once the butter has melted, add the mushrooms and onion. Sauté the mixture for 6 to 7 minutes, until the mushrooms are brown and the onion is tender. Set this mixture aside.

In a medium pot over high heat, bring the broth to a simmer. Add the buckwheat, salt, black pepper, coriander, paprika and the mushroom-onion mixture. Stir to combine the ingredients, then cover the pot and reduce the heat to low. Cook the buckwheat according to package instructions (most call for approximately 15 minutes). Do not uncover the pot, as the buckwheat needs to steam.

Fluff the buckwheat with a fork and serve. Buckwheat can be stored in the refrigerator for up to 1 week.

HEARTY SALADS AND PICKLED VEGETABLES

Eastern European salads are typically hearty and filling. You won't find too many recipes that are made with leafy greens or spinach. Instead, most salads are made with hearty root vegetables or fresh veggies straight from the garden, like tomatoes and cucumbers. Summers in Eastern Europe and Russia are short, meaning that those fresh garden salads are only around for a short while! Root vegetables such as beets, carrots and potatoes are more readily available, easier to store and last longer. In this chapter, you'll find the classics like Olivier Potato Salad (page 103) and Layered Holiday Salad (page 104), as well as Korean Carrot Salad (page 111) and plenty of recipes with beets.

Pickling vegetables and mushrooms is a great way to preserve fresh produce. Pickled salads and pickled mushrooms are very popular in Eastern Europe and pair perfectly with heavier meat and potato dishes. These pickled vegetables are often served on the side of meals instead of salads—they complement the food and are very refreshing, so be sure to try the pickled veggies in this chapter!

OLIVIER POTATO SALAD

Салат Оливье ✦ Salat Oliv'ye

Olivier potato salad is the iconic Eastern European version of American potato salad. It's made with loads of veggies, pickles, peas, eggs and even kielbasa to add some meaty flavor. It's an everyday staple and is also enjoyed on Christmas and New Year's Eve and during weddings, holidays and birthday parties. If there is dinner to be served, you better bet there will be Olivier salad!

The original Olivier salad recipe served in the 1860s in Moscow contained caviar. For a special occasion, garnish the salad with sliced hard-boiled eggs and spoonfuls of salmon roe.

YIELD: 10 CUPS (3.4 KG)

Place the potatoes and carrots in a large pot and cover them with water. Bring the potatoes and carrots to a boil over high heat and cook until the vegetables are tender, about 15 minutes. Transfer the vegetables to a tray and allow them to cool completely.

Meanwhile, bring another large pot of salted water to a boil over high heat. Add the eggs. Cook them for 8 minutes, then transfer them to an ice bath to cool. Once cooled, peel the eggs and set them aside.

Once the potatoes, carrots and eggs are cool, dice them—along with the pickles and sausage—into pea-sized pieces and place them in a large bowl. Add the sweet peas.

Dress the salad with the mayonnaise and sour cream and add the salt and dill. Add the shallot (if using) when you are ready to serve.

QUICK TIP: To cut down on prep time, you can cook the potatoes, carrots and eggs in advance of preparing the rest of the ingredients.

4 large potatoes

5 large carrots

8 large eggs

10 medium dill pickles

1½ cups (210 g) diced beef kielbasa or bologna

1 cup (150 g) canned or frozen sweet peas, drained or thawed

¾ cup (165 g) mayonnaise

½ cup (120 g) sour cream

1 tbsp (15 g) salt

2 tbsp (4 g) finely chopped fresh dill

1 shallot, diced into pea-sized pieces (optional)

LAYERED HOLIDAY SALAD

Салат Шуба ✦ Salat Shuba

This incredible layered salad is hiding a secret under all those colorful layers: herring! Of all the dishes in this cookbook, this is one that I have to say might be an acquired taste. I personally love this salad because of the unique flavors—the sweet beets and carrots, hearty potatoes and marinated herring come together in an incredible symphony. In Ukraine and Russia, this salad is usually enjoyed around Christmas and New Year's. It keeps very well in the refrigerator and can be made ahead of time for a dinner party.

YIELD: 8 TO 10 SERVINGS

Place the potatoes and carrots in a large pot and the beets in another large pot. Cover the vegetables completely with water, then salt the water and bring it to a boil over high heat. Cook for 20 to 30 minutes, until the vegetables are fork-tender (the exact cooking time will depend on the size of the root vegetables, so check them often). Remove them from the water and let them cool completely before handling.

Bring a small pot of salted water to a boil over high heat. Add the eggs and cook them for 9 to 10 minutes. Once done, place them in an ice bath. Once cooled, peel the eggs and set them aside.

Once the potatoes, carrots and beets have cooled, use a paring knife to remove the skins. Grate each ingredient into three separate large bowls and season each lightly with salt.

In a medium bowl, combine the mayonnaise, sour cream and 1 tablespoon (2 g) of the dill. Whisk until the mixture is smooth. Reserve 2 tablespoons (30 ml) of the spread in a small bowl for later.

To assemble the salad, line the inside of a 6-inch (15-cm) round pan with plastic wrap. Layer the salad like so: Spread the beets in an even layer, followed with one-third of the mayonnaise spread. Next, layer the carrots and potatoes, adding the remaining mayonnaise spread between each layer. Add an even layer of the onion, followed by the herring.

Compress the salad *lightly* from the top, then invert the salad onto a serving tray or plate and remove the plastic. Spread the reserved 2 tablespoons (30 ml) of the mayonnaise spread over the beets. Grate the eggs over the top and garnish the salad with the pomegranate arils (if using) and remaining 1 tablespoon (2 g) of dill. The salad may be served right away but is best served after being chilled for 2 to 3 hours.

2 large russet potatoes

3 to 4 large carrots

2 to 3 large beets

Salt, as needed

2 large eggs

¾ cup (165 g) mayonnaise

¼ cup (60 g) sour cream

2 tbsp (4 g) finely chopped fresh dill, divided

1 small onion, diced

12 oz (336 g) oil-marinated herring, drained and diced into bite-size pieces

¼ cup (175 g) pomegranate arils (optional)

QUICK TIPS: Make sure to use herring that is marinated in oil; do not use herring pickled in a white wine sauce.

For a different variation of this recipe, try using smoked salmon instead of the marinated herring.

BEET POTATO SALAD WITH SAUERKRAUT

Винегрет ✤ Vinigret

Beets are an integral part of Ukraine's cuisine, and this beet potato salad is a great example of that fact. This easy and delicious salad is similar to a regular potato salad but boasts beets and a bit of sauerkraut for zesty flavor. There are two different ways of dressing this salad: The most popular method is to dress it with olive oil. The second option is to create a creamy version using mayonnaise and sour cream. Both dressings are delicious!

YIELD: 10 CUPS (3.3 KG)

The beets, potatoes and carrots need to be cooked or baked until they are fork-tender (this can be done ahead of time.) To boil the vegetables, place the potatoes and carrots in a large pot and the beets in another large pot. Cover the vegetables completely with water and bring it to a boil over high heat. Cook until the vegetables are fork-tender, 20 to 30 minutes (the exact cooking time will depend on the size of the root vegetables, so check them often). Remove them from the water and let them cool completely before handling.

To bake the vegetables, preheat the oven to 375°F (191°C). Place the potatoes and carrots on a large baking tray and cover the tray with foil. Wrap the beets in a foil pack, as they need more concentrated heat to cook faster. Bake the potatoes and carrots for 30 minutes and the beets for 45 to 60 minutes. Remove the vegetables from the oven and let them cool completely before handling.

Once the root vegetables have cooled, use a paring knife to gently peel the carrots, potatoes and beets. Dice all the vegetables into pea-size pieces.

In a large bowl, combine the potatoes, carrots, beets, peas, sauerkraut and pickles. Season the salad with the dill and salt and dress it with the oil. Add the shallot immediately before serving.

QUICK TIP: *To make a creamy version of this salad, omit the olive oil and add ½ cup (110 g) of mayonnaise and ¼ cup (60 g) of sour cream instead.*

4 to 5 medium russet potatoes

4 to 5 large carrots

4 to 5 large beets

1 cup (150 g) canned or frozen sweet peas, drained or thawed

½ cup (75 g) sauerkraut

½ cup (75 g) diced dill pickles

2 to 3 tbsp (4 to 6 g) finely chopped fresh dill

1 tbsp (15 g) salt

½ cup (120 ml) extra-virgin olive oil

1 shallot, diced

TOMATO AND CUCUMBER SUMMER SALAD

Помидорный Салат ✤ Pomidorniy Salat

This simple and refreshing tomato and cucumber salad is the quintessential Slavic summer salad. It can be served for breakfast, lunch and dinner as a side to just about anything. I love to make this salad with sweet, summer heirloom tomatoes and crispy Persian cucumbers. This recipe yields about six servings but can be increased for larger groups.

YIELD: 6 CUPS (1.4 KG)

In a large bowl, combine the cucumbers, tomatoes, green onions and dill.

Immediately before serving, season the salad with the salt and toss the salad with the oil and lemon juice.

10 to 12 small Persian or pickling cucumbers, thickly sliced

3 to 4 medium tomatoes, cut into bite-size pieces

4 green onions, diced

2 tbsp (4 g) finely chopped fresh dill

Salt, as needed

¼ cup (60 ml) extra-virgin olive oil

1 tbsp (15 ml) fresh lemon juice or distilled white vinegar

KOREAN CARROT SALAD

Морква По-Корейски ✤ Morkva po Koreski

If you love a crunchy, delicious salad, you're going to fall in love with this spicy carrot salad. This Russian-Korean salad recipe was inspired by kimchi from neighboring Korea. Since savoy cabbage is not readily available in Russia or Eastern Europe, the cabbage was eventually replaced with just carrots and the ingredients were changed and simplified. This version doesn't taste like kimchi because it has its own unique flavors—garlic, onion, coriander and cilantro. It's an amazing side dish for many meat dishes, especially grilled meats.

The traditional recipe is made with finely julienned carrots. If you don't have a julienne grater, slice the carrots as thinly as possible or use the large section of a box grater.

YIELD: 6 TO 7 CUPS (300 TO 350 G)

¼ cup (60 ml) sunflower or grapeseed oil

1 small sweet onion, diced

½ tsp ground coriander

½ tsp paprika

½ to 1 tsp red pepper flakes

6 to 7 large carrots

2 to 2½ tsp (10 to 13 g) salt

1 tbsp (15 ml) distilled white vinegar

¼ cup (8 g) coarsely chopped fresh cilantro

6 cloves garlic, pressed

1 tsp ground black pepper

Preheat a large skillet over medium heat. Add the oil and onion. Reduce the heat to medium-low and cook the onion for about 10 minutes, until it's translucent but not brown. If the onion starts to brown, reduce the heat immediately. Add the coriander, paprika and red pepper flakes and cook for 30 seconds. Remove the skillet from the heat and allow the oil to infuse and cool while you complete the following step.

Peel the carrots, then use a julienne grater to grate the carrots into a large bowl. Season the carrots with the salt. Add the vinegar, then massage the carrots with your hands for about 1 minute.

Add the cilantro to the salad, then add the cooled onion mixture, garlic and black pepper. Massage the salad again until the carrots are well coated and seasoned. Adjust the seasonings as needed.

For best results, allow the salad to stand at room temperature for about 30 minutes prior to serving. Alternatively, cover the salad and refrigerate it overnight.

CABBAGE AND CUCUMBER SALAD

Салат с Капустой ✤ Salat s Kapustoy

Cabbage is an important vegetable in Eastern European cuisine, just like beets and potatoes. This refreshing and crunchy summer salad is bound to become a favorite! It is best with fresh and sweet summer cabbage or softer savoy cabbage. Load it up with sliced cucumbers and you've got the perfect salad for any meal. I like to add toasted almonds for an extra bit of crunch and flavor.

YIELD: 8 TO 10 CUPS (2.7 TO 3.4 KG)

1 small head green cabbage, thinly sliced

10 to 12 Persian cucumbers or 2 large English cucumbers, thickly sliced

3 green onions, diced

2 tbsp (4 g) finely chopped fresh dill

¼ cup (28 g) slivered almonds, toasted

¼ cup (60 ml) extra-virgin olive oil

2 tbsp (30 ml) distilled white vinegar

Salt, as needed

Place the cabbage in a large bowl and add the cucumbers, green onions, dill and almonds. Pour the oil and vinegar over the salad. Season the salad with the salt. Toss the salad and serve.

QUICK TIP: If you are making this salad ahead of time, combine the cabbage, cucumbers, dill, green onion and almonds in a large bowl, then cover and refrigerate the salad. Add the oil, vinegar and salt immediately before tossing and serving.

ZESTY RADISH AND DILL SALAD

Редисочный Салат ✤ Redisochniy Salat

This radish salad is made with just a few ingredients but really captures the flavors of Eastern Europe with plenty of dill and green onion. This salad recipe is especially delicious with farm-fresh radishes—they have a sweeter taste to them. Try adding sliced cucumbers for more variety.

YIELD: 4 CUPS (960 G)

Place the radishes in a large bowl and add the dill, green onions, oil, vinegar and salt. Toss the ingredients together until the radishes are well coated.

Serve this salad with the bread on the side shortly after dressing the radishes. If you are making this recipe ahead of time, combine the radishes, dill and green onions but do not dress it until you are ready to serve.

QUICK TIP: To make quick work of cutting the radishes, use a mandoline slicer.

2 to 3 bundles red radishes, washed, trimmed and thinly sliced (see Quick Tip)

¼ cup (8 g) finely chopped fresh dill

3 green onions (white and green parts), finely chopped

2 tbsp (30 ml) extra-virgin olive oil

2 tbsp (30 ml) distilled white vinegar

Salt, as needed

Bread, as needed

CREAMY BEET SALAD

Салат из Свеклы ✤ Salat s Svekli

Beets are a staple vegetable in Ukraine and used for many dishes, from soups to salads. My mom used to grow a large patch of beets just so we could enjoy this simple salad year-round! The combination of sweet beets with zesty garlic gives this creamy salad a unique and delicious flavor. I like to enjoy this recipe as a side salad with other dishes or use it as an appetizer spread on French bread. This salad can also be made with walnuts for added texture.

YIELD: 3 TO 4 CUPS (720 TO 960 G)

4 to 5 large beets (see Quick Tip)

1½ tsp (8 g) salt, plus more as needed, divided

½ cup (110 g) mayonnaise

8 to 10 cloves garlic, pressed, plus more as needed

2 tbsp (4 g) finely chopped fresh dill

¼ cup (30 g) finely chopped walnuts (optional)

Wash the beets and scrub away any dirt, but do not peel them. Cut any extra-large beets in half.

The beets now need to be baked or boiled until they are tender. To bake the beets, preheat the oven to 400°F (204°C). Place the beets on a large baking sheet, season them with the salt as needed and cover the baking sheet tightly with foil. Bake the beets for 40 to 50 minutes, until they are tender. To boil the beets, place them in a large pot and cover them with water. Season the water with the salt and cook the beets over medium heat until they are tender, about 30 minutes.

Remove the beets from the oven or the boiling water and allow them to cool. Once the beets are cool enough to handle, use a paring knife to remove the skins. Grate the beets into a large bowl.

Add the remaining 1½ teaspoons (8 g) of salt, mayonnaise, garlic and dill. For a zestier salad, add more garlic. Add the walnuts (if using). Use a spatula to combine all the ingredients. Cover and store any leftovers in the refrigerator.

QUICK TIP: The beets can be cooked ahead of time and stored in the refrigerator. Don't want to wait for the beets to cook? Use store-bought precooked beets!

PICKLED CABBAGE AND VEGGIE SALAD

Салат Квашеная Капуста ✦ Salat Kvashenaya Kapusta

This old-world Ukrainian recipe was passed down to my mom from a dear friend and neighbor more than twenty years ago, and our family has enjoyed it ever since! A refreshing pickled salad, it is made with summer cabbage, bell peppers, mushrooms, zucchini and carrots. The pickling juice requires just a few ingredients and does its work quickly, so this salad is ready to enjoy the next day. Once pickled and ready, this salad can stand in the refrigerator for weeks. Enjoy the salad by itself or as a side.

YIELD: 10 TO 12 CUPS (3.4 TO 4.1 KG)

To make the salad, use a paring knife to cut away the hard, fibrous core of the cabbage. Then use a large knife to carefully cut the cabbage into quarters. Slice each quarter into ½-inch (13-mm) thick slices.

Assemble the salad in a large stainless-steel bowl or pot. First, add the peppercorns, dill and garlic. Next, add a layer of cabbage followed by a layer of the bell peppers, celery, zucchini, mushrooms, carrots and jalapeño (if using). Continue alternating the cabbage and vegetables, pressing the vegetables together gently.

To make the pickling juice, combine the water, vinegar, oil, sugar and salt in a large pot over high heat. Once the mixture comes to a boil, remove it from the heat and let it stand for 4 to 5 minutes before pouring it over the arranged salad.

To ensure that all the vegetables will stay submerged in the pickling juice, place a plate over the salad and place a heavy object, such as a jar filled with water, on top of the plate. Allow the salad to stand at room temperature for about 6 hours, until it has completely cooled. Once it has cooled, store the salad in the refrigerator overnight.

The salad can be served as soon as the next day. The salad can be kept in the stainless-steel pot or bowl or can be transferred to glass jars. If you prefer to store the salad in jars, first transfer the vegetables to a jar, packing them tightly, then pour in the pickling juice until the jar is full.

SALAD

1 large green cabbage

10 to 15 black peppercorns

2 tbsp (4 g) finely chopped fresh dill

6 cloves garlic, thinly sliced

1 to 2 large red bell peppers, cubed

2 medium ribs celery, thinly sliced

1 to 2 medium zucchini, cubed

10 white mushrooms, thickly sliced

2 large carrots, thickly sliced

1 large jalapeño, thinly sliced (optional)

PICKLING JUICE

8 cups (1.9 L) water

1 cup (240 ml) apple cider vinegar

½ cup (120 ml) extra-virgin olive oil

½ cup (100 g) sugar

¼ cup (60 g) salt

QUICK PICKLED TOMATOES AND CUCUMBERS

Малосольные Огурцы и Помидоры ✤ Malosol'niye Ogurtsi i Pomidori

When you have buckets full of cucumbers and tomatoes from your garden, what do you do? Use this recipe! This easy pickling recipe has been in my family for generations. It was a childhood favorite of mine and is still one of my favorite ways to preserve garden vegetables. Plus, the flavor is incredible—the cucumbers and tomatoes take on a zesty and refreshing flavor. Serve these vegetables with grilled meats and heavier rice or potato dishes. I recommend using cocktail, pickling or Persian cucumbers and cherry tomatoes for this recipe.

YIELD: 4 LBS (1.8 KG)

In a small bowl, combine the peppercorns, dill, mustard seeds, dill seeds and coriander seeds. Divide the mixture evenly between two (1-quart [960-ml]) sanitized glass jars (see Quick Tip). Add 2 bay leaves and 3 cloves garlic to each jar.

Arrange the cucumbers and tomatoes in the jars, packing them loosely.

In a large measuring cup, combine the water, salt and sugar. Stir until the salt and sugar are completely dissolved, about 1 minute. Pour the pickling juice over the packed vegetables, filling the jars to the top.

Cover the jars with a small square of cheesecloth and use a rubber band to keep it in place. Keep the vegetables at room temperature in a dark area for 1 day, allowing the fermenting process to start. After 1 day, loosely close the jars with lids and keep the pickles in the refrigerator for up to 2 weeks.

QUICK TIP: Sanitize the jars by pouring about ½ cup (120 ml) of boiling water into each jar, swirling it around and pouring it out.

1 tsp black peppercorns

¼ cup (8 g) finely chopped fresh dill

½ tsp mustard seeds

½ tsp dill seeds

½ tsp coriander seeds

4 dried bay leaves

6 cloves garlic, thinly sliced

2 lbs (900 g) Persian or pickling cucumbers, halved or quartered

2 lbs (900 g) small tomatoes

4 cups (960 ml) cold water

2 tbsp (30 g) salt

1 tsp sugar

PICKLED MUSHROOMS

Маринованные Грибы ❧ Marenovoniye Griby

Eastern Europeans love their veggies pickled, and mushrooms are no exception! In fact, picking wild mushrooms is considered a fun weekend activity for the entire family. Pickled mushrooms are typically served as a salad side dish alongside meats or enjoyed on their own. This quick and easy recipe for pickled mushrooms can be made with a variety of mushrooms. Since wild mushrooms aren't readily available, I make this recipe most often with store-bought portobello mushrooms. Chanterelle mushrooms are my favorite when they are in season.

YIELD: 2 QUARTS (1.9 L)

Prepare one (2-quart [1.9-L]) glass jar with a lid or two (1-quart [960-ml]) glass jars with lids by washing them thoroughly with hot water. In a small ramekin, combine the peppercorns, mustard seeds, onion, garlic, bay leaves and red pepper flakes. If you are using one jar, add everything to one jar; otherwise, divide the ingredients equally between the jars.

Clean the mushrooms thoroughly and slice large mushrooms into halves or quarters. Pack the mushrooms gently but tightly into the prepared jars.

In a medium pot over medium heat, combine the water, vinegar, salt, sugar, oil and lemon juice. Bring the mixture to a simmer, then pour the hot liquid over the mushrooms, filling the jars to the top.

The mushrooms need to stay submerged in the pickling juice. Place a small ramekin over the mushrooms to keep them covered. Allow the pickling juice to cool completely at room temperature, then close the jar and keep the mushrooms in the refrigerator. The mushrooms can be served as soon as the next day and will keep well for up to 2 weeks in the refrigerator.

12 to 15 black peppercorns

2 tsp (6 g) mustard seeds

¼ cup (40 g) finely chopped sweet onion

6 cloves garlic, sliced

2 dried bay leaves

½ tsp red pepper flakes

1 lb (450 g) portobello, chanterelle or shimeji mushrooms

4 cups (960 ml) water

¼ cup (60 ml) distilled white vinegar

2 tbsp (30 g) salt

1 tbsp (13 g) sugar

2 tbsp (30 ml) canola oil

Juice from ½ lemon

TRADITIONAL SAUERKRAUT

Квашеная Капуста ❖ Kvashanaya Kapusta

Sauerkraut is an important dish for many cultures—and that goes for Eastern Europe as well. An old Polish saying goes, "Where there is beet soup and sauerkraut, there is plenty." This version of fermented cabbage is made with grated carrots, which add a bit of sweetness to the recipe. Use this sauerkraut recipe for other dishes in this book, such as my Braised Cabbage and Chicken (page 67), Braised Cabbage and Mushroom Piroshki (page 18) and Beet Potato Salad with Sauerkraut (page 107).

YIELD: 4 CUPS (600 G)

1 large head green cabbage

2 to 3 large carrots, grated

1 tsp dill seeds

1 tbsp (15 g) salt

1 tsp sugar

Using a large knife or a mandoline slicer, cut the cabbage into thin pieces about 1 inch (2.5 cm) in length. Place the cabbage in a large bowl and add the carrots, dill seeds, salt and sugar.

Using gloved hands, combine all the ingredients together until the mixture is uniform. Massage the cabbage for 4 to 5 minutes, until it's tender.

Thoroughly wash and rinse one (1-quart [960-ml]) glass jar with a lid. Stuff the cabbage mixture into the jar, compressing the mixture (the entire amount should fit easily into the jar).

As the cabbage is stuffed in the jar, it will begin to release juices. Place a small glass ramekin or other small, heavy object over the packed cabbage. This will allow the juices to rise to the top and cover the cabbage.

Cover the jar loosely with cheesecloth and use a rubber band to keep it in place. Allow the sauerkraut to stand at room temperature in a dark area for at least 3 days. Make sure the cabbage stays submerged under the pickling juice at all times. After 3 days, cover the jar with a lid and store the sauerkraut in the refrigerator for up to 1 month.

BELOVED DESSERTS, DRINKS AND OLD-WORLD PASTRIES

The following recipes showcase classic, old-world desserts that have been passed down through the generations. This chapter is especially nostalgic for me as it includes so many special and memorable recipes, like my mom's Apricot Butter Horns (page 149), refreshing Strawberries and Cream Parfait (page 157) and special holiday recipes like Easter Bread (page 131). To this day, the aroma of Apple Piroshki (page 144) in the oven takes me right back to my parents' kitchen. I'm also sharing my grandmother's recipe for Sweet Cheese Pancakes (page 140), which she always made for us when we came over. And I've always loved the sweet and magical zefir, or Fruit Marshmallow (page 139). Turn to this varied collection of dessert recipes for everyday treats and enjoy the decadent cake recipes on special occasions.

KIEV CAKE

Киевский Торт ✤ Kievskiy Tort

Here is my take on the famous Kiev cake, also known as hazelnut meringue cake. The original Kiev cake was created in 1956 and was wildly popular in the USSR. You can still buy the original cake in stores, even in the United States! This stunning Ukrainian cake recipe is made with simple sponge cake that is heightened with hazelnut liqueur, chocolate-hazelnut filling, silky French buttercream frosting and crunchy hazelnut meringue. The meringue is baked slowly, resulting in a crunchy and airy layer dotted with hazelnuts. All those layers, textures and flavors come together to create an unforgettable cake.

YIELD: 12 TO 16 SERVINGS

Note that the meringue layer takes a while to bake and can be prepared up to 3 days ahead of time. To make the meringue, preheat the oven to 230°F (110°C) and line the bottom and sides of a 9-inch (23-cm) springform pan with parchment paper.

Place the egg whites, sugar and cream of tartar in the very clean bowl of a stand mixer. (Save the egg yolks for the French buttercream.) Whip the mixture on high speed for 6 to 7 minutes, until very stiff and glossy peaks form. Add the vanilla and hazelnut extracts and whip again for 1 minute.

Gently fold in the hazelnuts by hand with a spatula. Transfer the meringue to the prepared pan, spreading it out evenly. Bake the meringue for 4½ hours. Do not open the oven door during the baking process or the meringue may crack. After 4½ hours, turn the oven off and allow the meringue to cool completely in the oven. (This step can be done overnight.) Once the meringue is cool, keep it stored in a cool, dry place; do not refrigerate it.

To make the sponge cake, preheat the oven to 350°F (177°C) and line the bottom of a 9-inch (23-cm) springform pan with parchment paper; do not grease the sides. Place the eggs, sugar and vanilla in the bowl of a stand mixer and whip on high speed for 7 to 8 minutes, until the mixture is thick, pale and fluffy. Combine the flour and baking powder in a small bowl and sift it, in small increments, into the egg mixture, folding the mixture gently and thoroughly by hand with a spatula after each addition. (Do not use the mixer for this step.)

(Continued)

MERINGUE

5 large egg whites

1 cup (200 g) granulated sugar

1 tsp cream of tartar

1 tsp pure vanilla extract

1 tsp pure hazelnut extract

1 cup (115 g) finely chopped hazelnuts

SPONGE CAKE

4 large eggs

⅔ cup (133 g) granulated sugar

1 tsp pure vanilla extract

1 cup (125 g) all-purpose flour

½ tsp baking powder

KIEV CAKE (CONTINUED)

Pour the cake batter into the prepared pan and bake the cake for 19 to 20 minutes, until the top of the sponge cake is a deep, golden-brown color. Remove the cake from the oven and let it cool completely before using a serrated knife to slice the cake in half horizontally to create two layers.

To make the French buttercream, place the egg yolks in the bowl of a stand mixer. Whip the egg yolks on high speed for about 5 minutes, until they are thick and pale. Meanwhile, pour the water into a small pot over medium heat and add the sugar. Cook the sugar syrup, undisturbed, for about 5 minutes, until the temperature reaches 238°F (114°C).

Reduce the mixer's speed to medium. Slowly pour the sugar syrup into the egg yolks. Once all the syrup has been added, increase the mixer's speed to high and whip the mixture for 5 to 7 minutes, until it is thick, pale and just warm to the touch. (Check the temperature by placing the inside of your wrist against the bottom of the bowl; it should be just warm.)

Begin adding the butter, 2 tablespoons (28 g) at a time, mixing well after each addition. Once all the butter has been added, scrape down the sides of the bowl and add the salt, vanilla, hazelnut extract and chocolate. Whip for 4 to 5 minutes, until the frosting is smooth and uniform.

Combine the water and hazelnut liqueur in a small bowl to form a simple syrup. Using a pastry brush, soak the tops of the sponge cake layers generously with the syrup.

Assemble the cake on a cake stand or cake decorating turntable: Begin with a sponge cake layer and spread a generous amount of the French buttercream over the layer. Next, add the meringue and top the meringue with the chocolate-hazelnut spread, followed by another layer of buttercream. Finish the cake with the second sponge cake layer and frost the top and sides of the cake with the remaining buttercream. Place the cake in the refrigerator for at least 30 minutes before adding the ganache.

To make the ganache, combine the milk, chocolate and shortening in a microwave-safe measuring cup. Heat for about 30 seconds in the microwave, just until the milk is hot. Let the chocolate stand for 2 to 3 minutes, then stir until the ganache is smooth, about 1 minute. Allow the ganache to cool down for at least 10 minutes, or until it is no longer hot. Gently pour the ganache over the chilled cake and use an offset spatula to nudge the chocolate down the sides. Garnish the top with any leftover buttercream (I use a French star tip for the dollops of frosting) and chopped hazelnuts.

Use a sharp serrated knife to cut the cake. For best results, refrigerate the cake overnight prior to cutting it.

FRENCH BUTTERCREAM

5 large egg yolks

⅓ cup (80 ml) water

1 cup (200 g) granulated sugar

2 cups (448 g) unsalted butter, softened

⅛ tsp salt

1 tsp pure vanilla extract

1 tsp pure hazelnut extract

1 cup (175 g) semisweet chocolate chips, melted and cooled slightly

SYRUP

½ cup (120 ml) water

½ cup (120 ml) hazelnut liqueur

CHOCOLATE-HAZELNUT SPREAD

1 cup (300 g) chocolate-hazelnut spread

CHOCOLATE GANACHE

¼ cup (60 ml) whole milk

1 cup (175 g) semisweet chocolate chips

1 tsp vegetable shortening

GARNISH

Chopped hazelnuts

EASTER BREAD

Кулич Пасхальный ✤ Kulich Pasxhal'niy

Kulich is a traditional Russian Orthodox Easter bread, made with dried fruits and a simple sugar glaze. The tradition behind this bread can be traced back millennia and has been practiced across Eastern Europe, not just in Russia. The bread is prepared for Easter, brought to the church to be blessed by the priest and then enjoyed after the service. Not only does this bread have deep cultural roots, it's also delicious! This buttery and flaky bread is sweet and moist and best enjoyed within a few days.

YIELD: 2 LOAVES

To make the bread, pour the milk into a large bowl, then whisk in the granulated sugar and sprinkle the yeast over the top. Allow this mixture to stand for about 5 minutes, then add the eggs and egg yolks, sour cream, butter and salt. Whisk the ingredients for 2 to 3 minutes, until the mixture is smooth.

Add 2 cups (250 g) of the flour and whisk for 2 to 3 minutes. Cover the bowl with a clean kitchen towel, place it over a pot filled with hot water and set it in a warm area of the kitchen to proof for 1½ hours, until the dough has doubled in size.

While the dough is proofing, place the dried fruit into a small bowl and fill it with warm water. Allow the dried fruit to soak until it is ready to be added to the dough.

Once the dough has proofed, continue adding the remaining 3⅔ cups (458 g) flour, forming a very soft and sticky dough. Transfer the dough to a generously floured work surface and knead the dough for 5 to 7 minutes, until it's smooth and elastic. Drain the dried fruit and add it and the white chocolate chips to the dough. Knead the dough again for 1 minute, until the dried fruit is evenly distributed.

(Continued)

BREAD

1 cup (240 ml) lukewarm whole milk

1 cup (200 g) granulated sugar

1 tbsp (9 g) active dry yeast

2 large eggs plus 2 large egg yolks

⅓ cup (80 g) sour cream

¾ cup (168 g) butter, melted

1 tsp salt

5⅔ cups (708 g) all-purpose flour, plus more as needed, divided

1 cup (120 g) mixed dried fruit (such as diced apricots, golden raisins, cranberries)

½ cup (88 g) white chocolate chips

EASTER BREAD (CONTINUED)

Prepare two pans for the dough. For the traditional round shape, use two (6 x 5–inch [15 x 13–cm]) Panettone paper baking molds, or shape a mold using a double layer of parchment paper: Line the bottom and sides of two (6-inch [15-cm]) round baking pans with parchment paper reaching 6 to 7 inches (15 to 18 cm) up the sides. Alternatively, line two (9 x 5–inch [23 x 13–cm]) loaf pans with parchment paper.

Divide the dough in half. Shape each half into round loaves and place them into the prepared pans. Allow the dough to proof for 1½ to 2 hours, until it has doubled in size.

Preheat the oven to 350°F (177°C). Bake the bread for 50 to 55 minutes, until it sounds hollow when tapped on the top. Remove the bread from the oven and let it cool for about 15 minutes before removing the loaves from the pans and transferring them to a wire rack to finish cooling.

To make the glaze, whisk together the confectioners' sugar, lemon juice and orange zest (if using) in a medium bowl. Pour the glaze over the bread, allowing it to drip down the sides. Garnish the top with the orange slices or rainbow sprinkles (if using). Allow the bread to cool completely before serving. Once it has cooled, keep it well covered to prevent it from drying out.

GLAZE

2 cups (250 g) confectioners' sugar

2 to 3 tbsp (30 to 45 ml) fresh lemon juice

Orange zest (optional)

Orange slices or rainbow sprinkles, for garnish (optional)

SWEET CHERRY PIEROGI

Вареники с Вишней ✤ Vareniki s Vishney

These sweet cherry pierogi are one of the most iconic Ukrainian desserts. They're usually made in the summertime with freshly picked sweet cherries or tart pie cherries. (They can also be made with a variety of other fillings, such as blueberries, strawberries, apples or even sweet cheese.) They do take a little patience and practice to make, but the taste is unforgettable.

YIELD: 40 PIEROGI

Whisk together the egg, water and sugar in a large bowl until smooth. Add 2 cups (250 g) of the flour in ½-cup (63-g) increments, until a soft and sticky ball of dough forms. Transfer the dough to a well-floured work surface and knead in the remaining ¾ cup (94 g) flour. Knead for 4 to 5 minutes, until the dough is smooth and elastic, adding more flour as needed. The dough should be very firm and slightly tacky. Wrap it tightly in plastic and place in the refrigerator for at least 1 hour.

Meanwhile, cut each pitted cherry in half (cut larger ones into quarters). Place them in a large bowl and then add ¼ cup (50 g) of the sugar and cornstarch and toss everything together.

Lightly flour a work surface and a large baking sheet. Divide the dough in half, and knead one half at a time for 1 minute while the other half rests. Flour the work surface again and roll the dough out using a rolling pin, until the dough is about ¹⁄₁₆ inch (2 mm) thick. The thinner the dough, the better. Use a 1½-inch (4-cm) round cookie cutter to cut out circles.

Strain any juices from the cherries, then place 1 heaping teaspoon of the cherry mixture in the center of each circle. Lightly flour your hands, then pinch the dough around the filling, creating a half-moon shape. (Try not to get any filling on the edges, as this will prevent the dough from sealing.) Place the pierogi on the prepared baking sheet. Repeat with the remaining dough and filling.

Bring a large pot of water to a boil over high heat. Add about 15 pierogi at a time to avoid overcrowding the pot. Cook them for 4 minutes, just until the dough is cooked. Use a slotted spoon to remove them and place them in a large bowl. Add the butter and remaining 2 tablespoons (26 g) of sugar to the cooked pierogi. Toss them in the butter and sugar, then serve warm.

DOUGH

1 large egg

¾ cup (180 ml) water

1 tbsp (13 g) granulated sugar

2¾ cups (344 g) all-purpose flour, plus more as needed, divided

FILLING

3 cups (675 g) fresh or thawed frozen sweet or sour pie cherries (see Quick Tips)

¼ cup (50 g) plus 2 tbsp (26 g) granulated sugar, divided

2 tbsp (18 g) cornstarch

¼ cup (60 ml) melted butter

QUICK TIPS: Fresh or frozen cherries will work for this recipe. Make sure to thaw frozen cherries and drain any liquids before using the cherries in the recipe. Commercial canned cherry pie filling will not work well in this recipe.

To freeze the pierogi, allow them to freeze solid on the baking sheet. Once they are frozen, transfer to freezer storage bags. They can be kept frozen for up to 6 months. When cooking frozen pierogi, increase the cooking time to 8 minutes.

RUSSIAN TEA COOKIES

Пряники ✤ Pryaniki

You'll find these cookies served and sold just about everywhere in Russia and Eastern Europe. As their name implies, they're meant to be enjoyed with tea or coffee. These simple, cake-like cookies are rolled, cut, baked and then coated with an egg-white glaze. You can find these cookies in a variety of flavors. My simple vanilla recipe is the perfect base for experimenting with other flavors (see Quick Tip).

YIELD: ABOUT 32 COOKIES

To make the cookies, combine the milk, egg yolks, butter, granulated sugar, vanilla and salt in a large bowl. Whisk for about 2 minutes, until the mixture is smooth. In a separate large bowl, combine 6 cups (750 g) of the flour with the baking soda and baking powder.

Add the flour mixture gradually to the batter, about 2 cups (250 g) at a time, and mix well with a spatula or wooden spoon after each addition. A soft and slightly sticky dough will form. Cover the bowl with plastic wrap and refrigerate the dough for at least 1 hour or up to overnight.

Preheat the oven to 350°F (177°C) and line two large baking sheets with parchment paper or silicone mats. Remove the dough from the refrigerator and sprinkle the remaining ⅓ cup (42 g) of flour over a work surface. Knead the dough gently for about 30 seconds, then use a well-floured rolling pin to roll the dough out into a 1-inch (2.5-cm) thick square or rectangle.

Use a 1½- to 2-inch (4- to 5-cm) round cookie cutter and cut out as many cookies as possible from the dough. Place the cookies on the prepared baking sheets about 1 inch (2.5 cm) apart. (The dough should only be re-kneaded once, otherwise it will be too tough.)

Bake the cookies for 21 to 22 minutes, until the bottoms are golden and the tops are slightly yellow. Transfer the cookies to a wire rack to cool.

To make the glaze, place the egg whites, confectioners' sugar, lemon juice and mint oil (if using) in the bowl of a stand mixer. Whip the mixture on high speed for 3 to 4 minutes, until the egg whites are thick and foamy.

When the cookies are just warm to the touch, they can be glazed. The cookies can be glazed two ways: by dipping them into the glaze and tapping off any excess or by brushing the glaze on with a pastry brush. Place the glazed cookies onto a wire rack and let the glaze set completely before storing them in an airtight container.

COOKIES

2 cups (480 ml) milk

2 large egg yolks

¼ cup (56 g) butter, melted

1½ cups (300 g) granulated sugar

1 tsp pure vanilla extract

½ tsp salt

6⅓ cups (790 g) all-purpose flour, divided

1 tsp baking soda

2 tsp (8 g) baking powder

GLAZE

2 large egg whites

2 cups (250 g) confectioners' sugar

1 tbsp (15 ml) fresh lemon juice

1 tsp food-grade mint oil (optional)

QUICK TIP: Here are some flavors to try: For an orange cookie, use the zest from 1 orange added to the cookie batter, plus 1 teaspoon of food-grade orange oil for the glaze. For a mint flavor, 1 teaspoon of food-grade mint oil or peppermint extract may be added to the cookie batter and 1 teaspoon to the glaze. For a spiced version, 1 teaspoon of ground cinnamon, ½ teaspoon of ground nutmeg and 1 teaspoon of ground ginger may be added to the cookie dough.

FRUIT MARSHMALLOW

Зефир ✤ Zefir

My parents would get these sweets for my siblings and I only on special occasions, and they were a treasured treat. These unique marshmallows are unlike anything you've ever had before. They're light, fluffy, fruity and simply melt in your mouth. These delicacies can be made with many fruit and berry flavors—they can even be dipped in chocolate! This recipe will work only with agar gelatin. I recommend searching for it online as it's not readily available in most stores.

YIELD: 30 BIG OR 60 SMALL MARSHMALLOWS

¾ cup (180 ml) cold water, divided

¼ cup (45 g) flavored gelatin powder (such as raspberry, strawberry, grape, cherry, orange or peach)

3 large egg whites

2 tsp (16 g) agar gelatin

2 cups (400 g) granulated sugar

1 tbsp (15 ml) fresh lemon juice

1 tsp fruit extract (the same flavor as the gelatin powder; optional)

Food coloring (optional)

1 cup (125 g) confectioners' sugar

Before starting the cooking process, prepare an extra-large pastry bag with a star tip (such as an Ateco #847 tip or a large French star tip). Line a clean 18 x 24–inch (45 x 60–cm) work surface with plastic wrap or 2 silicone mats.

In a small microwave-safe measuring cup, combine ¼ cup (60 ml) of the cold water with the gelatin powder. Microwave it for 1 to 1½ minutes, stirring frequently, until the gelatin is completely dissolved. Set aside.

Place the egg whites in the bowl of a stand mixer and whip them on high speed for about 2 minutes, until soft peaks form.

Pour the remaining ½ cup (120 ml) of water into a medium pot over medium heat. Add the agar gelatin. Cook this mixture, stirring frequently with a rubber spatula, until the mixture thickens, about 3 minutes. Begin adding the sugar gradually, about ½ cup (100 g) at a time, stirring just until it's absorbed, then do not stir again. Attach a candy thermometer to the side of the pot and, once the mixture comes to a rolling, foaming boil, cook it until the temperature reaches 230°F (110°C), about 3 minutes.

Turn the stand mixer on to medium speed and slowly pour the hot syrup into the egg whites. Add the dissolved gelatin mixture. Increase the speed to high speed and whip the mixture for 4 to 6 minutes, until the meringue starts to stiffen. Add the lemon juice and the extract and food coloring (if using), and whip for 30 seconds.

Working quickly, transfer the marshmallow to the prepared pastry bag. Pipe dollops of meringue onto the prepared work surface. The marshmallows will begin setting almost immediately. Allow the marshmallows to stand for 30 minutes, then sprinkle them with the confectioners' sugar using a fine-mesh sifter. Allow the marshmallows to set for at least 2 hours at room temperature. Once set, gently lift them off the plastic wrap and store them in an airtight container at room temperature for 1 week.

SWEET CHEESE PANCAKES

Сырники ✧ Sirniki

This easy and delicious recipe for sweet cheese pancakes is particularly special to me. My grandmother Yuliya would always have either cabbage-filled piroshki or these sirniki for my family when we came over. This recipe tastes exactly like the ones she used to make for us! Making these in my kitchen, on the opposite side of the globe from where she was born, really puts into perspective how far I have come. These easy cheese pancakes are traditionally made with quark, but large-curd cottage cheese works beautifully and it's readily available. Sirniki are great enjoyed while warm, in the morning for breakfast or as an afternoon snack.

YIELD: ABOUT 15 PANCAKES

3 lbs (1.4 kg) large-curd cottage cheese

⅓ cup (67 g) granulated sugar

1 large egg plus 1 large egg yolk

1 tsp pure vanilla extract

½ cup (180 g) farina

½ cup (60 g) dried cranberries or raisins

2 tbsp (16 g) all-purpose flour

¼ cup (56 g) unsalted butter, divided

Fruit jams (any varieties), as needed

Sour cream, as needed

2 tbsp (16 g) confectioners' sugar, for dusting (optional)

Line a large, fine-mesh strainer with a large piece of cheesecloth. Place the cottage cheese into the strainer and rinse the cheese under cold water until just the curds remain. Lift the cheesecloth out of the strainer and wring the curds as dry as possible. The less moisture, the better.

Place the cheese curds into a large bowl. Add the sugar, egg and egg yolk, vanilla, farina and cranberries. Use a spatula to fold the ingredients until the mixture is uniform, about 1 minute. Allow the mixture to rest for 15 minutes, so that the farina can absorb moisture and expand.

Place the flour in a small bowl. Using a ¼-cup (60-g) measuring cup, scoop out the dough for each pancake. Press the dough together to form a ball, then roll it lightly in the flour. Flatten the ball into a 2½-inch (6-cm) puck shape.

Preheat a large nonstick skillet over low heat. Line a large baking sheet with paper towels. Add 2 tablespoons (28 g) of the butter and allow it to melt. To avoid overcrowding the skillet, fry the pancakes in two batches, adding more butter to the skillet as needed. Do not increase the heat, as cooking the pancakes over low heat is crucial to allow the insides to cook.

Transfer the cooked pancakes to the prepared baking sheet to absorb the excess butter. Allow the pancakes to cool for at least 10 minutes before serving them warm with the jams and sour cream on the side. Dust the pancakes with confectioners' sugar, if desired.

QUICK TIP: These cheese pancakes can be prepared ahead of time and store very well. The cheese mixture can be prepared the night before and stored in the refrigerator. The pancakes can also be fried, then cooled and stored in an airtight container.

SOUR CREAM APPLE PANCAKES

Оладушки с Яблоками ✤ Oladushki s Yablokami

Pancakes of all types are popular in Eastern Europe, and they can be served for breakfast, lunch and dinner. These fluffy and delicious pancakes can be enjoyed for breakfast or as a dessert with hot tea. I love the texture of these apple-filled pancakes—the buttermilk and sour cream make them extra fluffy and the diced apples add great texture and flavor. Serve these warm with extra sour cream on the side or with a side of fruit preserves.

YIELD: 16 TO 18 PANCAKES

½ cup (120 ml) buttermilk

1 cup (240 g) sour cream, divided

½ cup (120 ml) milk

2 large eggs

¼ cup (50 g) granulated sugar

1 tsp pure vanilla extract

2¼ cups (280 g) all-purpose flour

1 tsp baking soda

2 large Granny Smith or Gala apples, diced

¼ cup (60 ml) canola or grapeseed oil, divided

Fruit preserves, for serving (optional)

2 tbsp (16 g) confectioners' sugar, for dusting (optional)

In a large bowl, combine the buttermilk, ½ cup (120 g) of the sour cream, milk, eggs, sugar and vanilla. Whisk until the batter is smooth and clump-free, about 2 minutes. In a medium bowl, combine the flour and baking soda. Sift the flour into the batter. Whisk the flour into the batter just until the batter is smooth, about 1 minute.

Add the apples and use a spatula to gently fold them into the batter.

Preheat a large nonstick skillet over medium heat and add 1 tablespoon (15 ml) of the oil. Once the oil is hot, add 2 tablespoons (30 ml) of the pancake batter to the skillet for each pancake. Cook the pancakes for about 2 minutes per side, turning them once the first side is golden brown. Add 1 tablespoon (15 ml) of oil for each new batch of pancakes.

Serve the pancakes warm, with the remaining ½ cup (120 g) of sour cream on the side, along with fruit preserves, if desired. Dust with confectioners' sugar for extra sweetness, if desired.

APPLE PIROSHKI

Яблочные Пирожки ✤ Yabluchniye Piroshki

These classic apple-filled piroshki are a much-loved version of sweet piroshki in Eastern Europe. This recipe brings back so many warm memories of my mother making these in the fall months with apples from our orchard. Now when I make them, I always think back to the days of cutting apples and learning how to shape these pastries in our little kitchen.

YIELD: 16 PIROSHKI

To make the dough, pour the milk into a large bowl, then whisk in the sugar and sprinkle the yeast over the milk. Let this mixture stand for 5 minutes, allowing the yeast to bloom. Add the salt, egg and butter and whisk for 2 minutes, until the mixture is smooth.

Begin adding the flour, 1 cup (125 g) at a time, to create a soft dough. Once a dough ball forms, transfer it to a lightly floured work surface and knead it for 4 to 5 minutes, until the dough is smooth and elastic but slightly sticky. Place the dough back into the bowl, cover with a tea towel and allow the dough to proof in a warm area for 1 hour, or until double in size.

Meanwhile, place the apples in a large pot over medium heat. Add 1 cup (240 ml) of the water, sugar, nutmeg, cinnamon and cranberries (if using). Simmer for 20 minutes, until the apples begin to soften and release their juices. If necessary, add more water in ¼-cup (60-ml) intervals. In a small ramekin, combine the cornstarch and remaining ¼ cup (60 ml) of water to create a slurry. Add the slurry to the apples. Cook the apples for about 1 minute, until the juices thicken. Remove the filling from the heat and allow it to cool.

Once the dough has proofed, lightly flour a work surface and line a large baking sheet with parchment paper or a silicone mat. Knead the dough again for 1 minute. Divide it into 16 pieces. For each piroshok, roll the dough out into a 6-inch (15-cm) circle that is ⅛ inch (3 mm) thick. Place about ⅓ cup (80 g) of the filling in the center of the dough circle. Lift the dough around the sides into the center of the circle and pinch it together, forming a pouch. Place the shaped piroshki on the prepared baking sheet, at least 2 inches (5 cm) apart. Set the piroshki aside to proof for 30 minutes.

Meanwhile, preheat the oven to 350°F (177°C). Before baking the piroshki, brush them with the beaten egg. Bake the piroshki for 24 to 26 minutes, or until the dough is golden brown. Remove the piroshki and allow them to cool on a wire rack. Serve them warm with any leftover filling or apple butter.

DOUGH

1½ cups (360 ml) lukewarm whole milk

½ cup (100 g) sugar

1 tbsp (9 g) active dry yeast

½ tsp salt

1 large egg

¼ cup (56 g) unsalted butter, melted

4¾ cups (594 g) all-purpose flour, plus more as needed

FILLING

7 to 8 large Granny Smith or Gala apples, peeled and diced

1¼ cups (300 ml) water, divided, plus more as needed

1 cup (200 g) sugar

¼ tsp ground nutmeg

½ tsp ground cinnamon

1 cup (125 g) fresh cranberries (optional)

¼ cup (36 g) cornstarch

FOR EGG WASH

1 large egg, beaten

QUICK TIP: For even more flavor, try adding fresh, in-season cranberries to the filling.

POPPY SEED ROLL

Рулет с Маком ✣ Roulet s Makom

This sweet yeast bread filled with poppy seeds is loved by everyone and is great for breakfast! It's light, fluffy and not too sweet. This recipe is the classic version, with just poppy seeds and sugar. The rolls can also be made with a combination of nuts, dried fruit, chocolate and even fruit preserves. The proofing process for the dough is a bit lengthy, which makes this recipe great for the weekend. Don't forget to soak the poppy seeds overnight for best results.

YIELD: 3 LOAVES

1 cup (125 g) poppy seeds

½ cup (120 ml) warm water

1 cup (240 ml) lukewarm whole milk

1¼ cups (250 g) granulated sugar, divided

1½ tbsp (14 g) instant dry yeast

1½ cups (336 g) unsalted butter, melted and slightly cooled

¼ tsp salt

3 large eggs plus 2 large egg yolks, divided

5 cups (625 g) all-purpose flour

Place the poppy seeds in a small bowl and add the water. Stir the seeds and water together and let the seeds stand while you are preparing the dough. (For best results, the seeds should soak overnight.)

Add the milk to a large bowl. Sprinkle ½ cup (100 g) of the sugar over the milk and stir, then sprinkle the yeast over the milk. Let the yeast proof for 5 minutes, then whisk for 1 minute until the yeast is dissolved.

Add the butter, salt, two of the eggs and the egg yolks to the milk. Whisk the mixture vigorously for 2 to 3 minutes, until the eggs are smooth.

Dust a work surface with flour. Begin adding the flour, 1 cup (125 g) at a time, to the milk mixture: Whisk it into the milk mixture at first, then switch to a spatula when the dough starts to pull together. The dough needs to be very soft and just slightly tacky but not too sticky. Transfer the dough to the work surface and knead the dough for 5 to 6 minutes, until it's smooth.

Place the dough in another large bowl, cover the bowl with a clean kitchen towel and let the dough proof in a warm area until it has doubled in size, about 1½ hours.

While the dough is proofing, finish preparing the poppy seed filling. Place the soaked seeds into a food processor, along with the remaining ¾ cup (150 g) of sugar. Pulse the seeds and sugar for 2 to 3 minutes, until a thick paste forms.

(Continued)

POPPY SEED ROLL (CONTINUED)

After the dough has proofed, lightly flour a work surface and line a large baking sheet with parchment paper or a silicone mat. Transfer the dough to the work surface and knead it for 1 minute. Divide the dough into three equal pieces and lightly flour the work surface and a rolling pin. Roll the dough out into a 12 x 18–inch (30 x 45–cm) rectangle. Spoon one-third of the poppy seed filling onto the dough, spreading it evenly to the edges. Starting at the short end of the dough, gently roll the dough into a log, creating a 12-inch (30-cm) long log. Repeat this process with the remaining dough and filling.

Preheat the oven to 375°F (191°C). Transfer the logs to the prepared baking sheet, placing them seam side down. Space the logs at least 3 inches (8 cm) apart. Cover the baking sheet with a clean kitchen towel and allow the dough to proof for about 45 minutes next to the preheating oven, until it has doubled in size.

After the dough has proofed, beat the remaining egg in a small bowl. Use a pastry brush to brush the beaten egg over each log. Bake the bread for 35 to 40 minutes, until the tops are a rich golden brown. Remove the rolls from the oven and allow them to cool on the baking sheet for at least 30 minutes. When you are ready to serve, slice the loaves into sections using a serrated knife. Once the bread has cooled, wrap it first in a clean tea towel and then with plastic, to prevent it from drying out, and store it at room temperature.

APRICOT BUTTER HORNS

Рогалики с Вареньем ❧ Rohaliki s Varenyem

I have so many warm memories associated with this buttery cookie recipe. My mom would make these often for the holidays or church gatherings and we would gather around our small kitchen to help her make at least a hundred cookies! This Polish recipe calls for yeast and yields very fluffy and flaky butter horns. The cookies can be made with a variety of fillings and flavors. Simply replace the apricot preserves with your choice of filling. My favorites are apple butter, apricot and pecan, raspberry, chocolate-hazelnut spread and strawberry. You can also use chocolate chips, toffee chips or a combination of finely chopped nuts with chocolate chips.

YIELD: 32 COOKIES

½ cup (120 ml) lukewarm whole milk

2 tbsp (26 g) granulated sugar

1 tbsp (9 g) active dry yeast

2 large eggs plus 1 large egg yolk

½ cup plus 2 tbsp (140 g) unsalted butter, melted

2 tbsp (30 g) sour cream

4 cups (500 g) all-purpose flour

1 cup (320 g) apricot preserves

1 cup (125 g) finely chopped pecans

1 cup (125 g) confectioners' sugar (optional)

Pour the milk in a large bowl, then whisk in the granulated sugar and sprinkle the yeast over the top. Allow the yeast to stand for 5 minutes. Whisk in the eggs and egg yolk, butter and sour cream; whisk for 2 to 3 minutes, until a smooth mixture forms.

Lightly flour a work surface. Slowly begin adding the flour, 1 cup (125 g) at a time, to the milk mixture, mixing well after each addition. The dough should be very soft but not sticky. Transfer the dough to the floured work surface and knead it for 4 to 5 minutes, until the dough is smooth.

Place the dough in a clean large bowl, cover the bowl with a clean kitchen towel and allow the dough to proof for about 1 hour, until it has doubled in size. Line a large baking sheet with parchment paper or a silicone mat.

Lightly flour a work surface. Once the dough has proofed, knead it again on the prepared work surface for about 30 seconds to flatten it, then divide it into four equal pieces. Roll out each piece of dough into a 10-inch (25-cm) circle. Spread ¼ cup (80 g) of the preserves evenly to the edges of the dough. Sprinkle the preserves with ¼ cup (31 g) of pecans. Use a sharp knife or pizza cutter to slice the circle into eight equal wedge-shape pieces. Carefully roll up each piece, tucking the edge underneath and place it onto the prepared baking sheet. Repeat this process for the remaining cookies.

(Continued)

APRICOT BUTTER HORNS (CONTINUED)

Alternatively, cut the dough circle into eight equal wedge-shape pieces, then add a dollop of preserves onto the wide end of the pieces. Press the dough around the filling, then roll it up. (Use this method for heftier fillings, such as jams, spreads and chocolate chips.)

Preheat the oven to 350°F (177°C). Allow the shaped cookies to proof on the baking sheet for at least 30 minutes, until they have doubled in size. Bake the cookies for 18 to 19 minutes, until they are golden brown.

If desired, toss the cookies in the confectioners' sugar. (This needs to be done as soon as the cookies come out of the oven, to ensure the sugar sticks.) Place the confectioners' sugar into a large bowl, then toss 2 to 3 hot cookies at a time, coating the cookies well. Gently tap off any excess sugar and place the cookies onto a wire rack to cool.

Allow the cookies to cool completely, then store them in an airtight container at room temperature.

SWEET CHEESE BUNS

Ватрушки ✦ Vatrushki

Buttery, flaky and sweet, these buns are known as vatrushki and are popular for good reason—they're not too sweet, they can be made in a variety of flavors and they're perfect with a cup of coffee or tea. The buns are made with a buttery yeast dough, then stuffed with a combination of quark cheese (or cottage cheese), cream cheese and various fillings, such as cherries, berries, raisins or chocolate chips.

YIELD: 16 BUNS

To make the dough, pour the milk into a large bowl, whisk in the sugar and then sprinkle the yeast over the top. Let the yeast proof for 5 minutes, then stir the mixture for 1 minute, until the yeast is dissolved. Add the butter, salt and eggs and egg yolks. Whisk vigorously for 2 to 3 minutes, until smooth. Begin adding the flour, 1 cup (125 g) at a time. Whisk it into the milk mixture at first, then switch to a spatula when the dough starts to pull together. The dough needs to be very soft and just slightly tacky but not too sticky. Transfer the dough to a floured work surface and knead for 5 to 6 minutes, until it's smooth. Place the dough in a clean bowl, cover with a clean kitchen towel and let it proof in a warm area until double in size, about 1½ hours.

Meanwhile, line a large, fine-mesh strainer with cheesecloth and add the cottage cheese. Rinse the cottage cheese under cold water until just the curds remain. Using the cheesecloth, carefully wring the cheese dry, leaving small, dry curds. Place them in a large bowl and add the cream cheese, one of the eggs, sugar, vanilla and lemon zest. At this point, you may add additional fillings if you'd like. Mix all the ingredients together.

Line two large baking sheets with parchment paper. Once the dough has proofed, divide it into sixteen equal pieces. Knead each piece of dough on a floured work surface into a uniform ball, then place them onto the prepared baking sheets, arranging the balls about 3 inches (8 cm) apart. Gently press each piece into a small disk and form a large well in the middle to hold the filling.

In a small bowl, beat the remaining egg. Place 1½ to 2 tablespoons (23 to 30 g) of the filling in the center of each bun, pressing it down gently. Brush the shaped buns with the beaten egg, then allow them to proof at room temperature for about 30 minutes.

Meanwhile, preheat the oven to 350°F (177°C). Bake the buns for 30 to 33 minutes, until the dough is golden brown. Remove from the oven and let them cool slightly on a wire rack before serving them warm.

DOUGH

1 cup (240 ml) lukewarm whole milk

½ cup (100 g) granulated sugar

1½ tbsp (14 g) active dry yeast

1½ cups (336 g) unsalted butter, melted and slightly cooled

¼ tsp salt

2 large eggs plus 2 large egg yolks

5 cups (625 g) all-purpose flour

FILLING

3 lbs (1.4 kg) large-curd cottage cheese

8 oz (224 g) cream cheese, softened

2 large eggs, divided

½ cup (100 g) granulated sugar

1 tsp pure vanilla extract

Zest from ½ lemon

CARAMEL WAFFLE ROLLS

Вафельные Трубочки ✤ Vafel'niye Trubochki

These crispy waffle rolls are filled with a creamy caramel frosting, and they're perfect with a cup of coffee or tea. This recipe is one of my husband's favorite desserts—and he doesn't even like sweets! In Eastern Europe, crispy waffle recipes come in a large variety: There are waffle cakes made with thin, delicate waffles; waffle cones filled with whipped cream frosting; or waffles filled with caramel, like these. This recipe does require either a krumkake, pizzelle or waffle cone machine, but the investment is worth it if you love caramel!

YIELD: ABOUT 30 WAFFLES

To make the waffles, melt the butter in a medium pot over medium heat. Once the butter has melted, add the milk and granulated sugar. Cook the mixture, stirring constantly until the sugar is dissolved, for about 2 minutes. The mixture does not need to boil.

Remove the mixture from the heat and add the eggs, vanilla and salt. Whisk for 1 minute, until the mixture is smooth, then add the flour. Whisk vigorously for 1 to 2 minutes, until the batter is completely smooth and clump-free.

Preheat a waffle cone machine or pizzelle machine to medium-high. Add 1½ to 2 tablespoons (23 to 30 ml) of batter per waffle, based on the machine's recommendation. Cook the waffles for 2½ to 3 minutes, until they are golden brown in color. Remove the hot waffle from the machine using a rubber spatula, then quickly roll it around a ½-inch (13-mm) dowel or roll of foil; the waffle needs to cool and set with an opening in the middle to accommodate the filling. Cool the waffle rolls completely on a wire rack.

Once the waffle rolls have cooled, prepare the filling. Place the butter in the bowl of a stand mixer and whisk on high speed for 3 to 4 minutes, until the butter is light and fluffy. (Alternatively, you may whisk the filling in a large bowl using a handheld mixer.) Add the dulce de leche, vanilla and salt and whisk again for 2 minutes, scraping down the sides of the bowl often. Add the confectioners' sugar and whisk for another 2 to 3 minutes, until the mixture is fluffy. If the filling is too thin, place the bowl in the refrigerator for 30 minutes, then whisk again for 1 minute.

Transfer the filling to a pastry bag fitted with a medium tip (such as an Ateco #843 tip). Pipe each waffle roll full of caramel filling from both sides. Keep the waffle rolls at room temperature, or refrigerate them if you are not serving them right away.

WAFFLES

½ cup (112 g) unsalted butter

1⅓ cups (320 ml) whole milk

1 cup (200 g) granulated sugar

2 large eggs

1 tsp pure vanilla extract

¼ tsp salt

2 cups (250 g) all-purpose flour

FILLING

1 cup (224 g) unsalted butter, softened at room temperature

1 (13-oz [364-g]) can dulce de leche

1 tsp pure vanilla extract

⅛ tsp salt

1 cup (125 g) confectioners' sugar

STRAWBERRIES AND CREAM PARFAIT

Клубника Со Сметаной ✤ Klubnika So Smetanoy

This recipe is made with exactly what the title implies—strawberries and sour cream! Sour cream is a staple ingredient in Eastern European cuisine, and this dessert recipe is no exception. When I was growing up, my family had a huge strawberry patch in our backyard. It was very fruitful, and we enjoyed this simple strawberry dessert almost every day during the summer months. The tart sour cream complements the sweet berries, resulting in a unique and delicious treat.

4 cups (576 g) fresh strawberries, halved

½ cup (100 g) granulated sugar (see Quick Tip)

½ cup (120 g) sour cream

1 tsp pure vanilla extract

YIELD: 5 CUPS (1.2 L)

Place the strawberries in a large bowl. Using a potato masher or a pastry blender, mash the strawberries into a sort of chunky puree. The puree shouldn't be too smooth.

Add the sugar, sour cream and vanilla and stir until well combined.

Leftovers can be stored in the refrigerator for 1 day.

QUICK TIP: *The amount of sugar can be reduced to your taste, or it can be omitted entirely.*

SWEET CHEESE CREPES

Налисники ✤ Nalisniki

These cheese-filled crepes are perfect with a cup of coffee in the morning or for dessert after dinner. Nalisniki are made with sweet crepes and filled with tvorog, a Russian cheese similar to cottage cheese but drier. Raisins and cranberries are also a popular addition to the filling. For this recipe, I use a combination of cottage and ricotta cheese, which are more accessible but have the same flavor as tvorog.

There are two different methods of preparation: pan-frying the crepes with butter or baking them with sour cream sauce. Both methods are delicious, and the crepes are great with a topping of fresh berries, berry jam or sour cream. These crepes are also great for making ahead of time and reheating when you are ready to enjoy them.

YIELD: 15 CREPES

To make the crepes, place the eggs, milk, butter, sugar, vanilla, salt and flour in a blender and pulse for 2 to 3 minutes, until a smooth batter forms. To prepare the batter without a blender, whisk together the eggs, milk, butter, sugar, vanilla and salt in a large bowl for 1 to 2 minutes, until the mixture is smooth. Sift the flour into the batter and whisk for 2 to 3 minutes, until the mixture is smooth.

Preheat a 9-inch (23-cm) nonstick crepe pan over medium heat. For each crepe, add ¼ cup (60 ml) of batter to the center of the pan and tilt it to spread the batter evenly. Cook the crepe for 1 minute on the first side, until the crepe batter is no longer shiny. Use a rubber spatula to turn the crepe over and cook it on the other side for 30 seconds. Stack the crepes on a wire rack to cool.

To make the filling, place the cottage cheese in a fine-mesh strainer lined with cheesecloth. Rinse the cheese under cold water, leaving just the cheese curds. Using the cheesecloth, wring the cheese curds dry (the less moisture, the better). Transfer the cottage cheese curds to a large bowl and add the ricotta cheese, sugar, vanilla and egg yolks. Mix the ingredients with a spatula for about 2 minutes, until they are well combined.

(Continued)

CREPES

4 large eggs

2 cups (480 ml) whole milk

¼ cup (56 g) butter, melted

¼ cup (50 g) granulated sugar

1 tsp pure vanilla extract

Pinch of salt

1⅔ cups (208 g) all-purpose flour

FILLING

1 lb (450 g) small-curd cottage cheese

1 lb (450 g) whole-milk ricotta cheese

½ cup (100 g) granulated sugar

1 tsp pure vanilla extract

2 large egg yolks

SWEET CHEESE CREPES (CONTINUED)

Place approximately 2 tablespoons (30 g) of the filling into the center of each crepe. Fold the sides of the crepe around the filling, then roll the crepe into a tight log (similar to an egg roll). Alternatively, spread the cheese evenly across the crepe and roll the crepe into an open-ended log.

To pan-fry the crepes, preheat a large, nonstick skillet over medium heat. Add 2 tablespoons (28 g) of the butter and allow it to melt. Fry 3 to 5 crepes at a time for 2 to 3 minutes per side. Add the remaining 4 tablespoons (56 g) of butter as needed.

To bake the crepes, preheat the oven to 375°F (191°C). Place the filled crepes in a medium baking dish. To make the sour cream sauce, combine the milk, sour cream and butter in a large measuring cup and whisk until the mixture is smooth. Pour the sauce over the assembled crepes. Cover the baking dish with foil and bake the crepes for 45 minutes. Remove the crepes and allow them to cool for at least 30 minutes before serving.

Serve the crepes warm with the sour cream, fresh berries and fruit preserves. Dust with the confectioners' sugar, if using. Reheat leftover crepes using the pan-frying method.

FOR FRYING

6 tbsp (84 g) butter

SOUR CREAM SAUCE

¼ cup (60 ml) milk

¼ cup (60 g) sour cream

¼ cup (56 g) unsalted butter, melted

FOR SERVING

Sour cream, as needed

Fresh berries, as needed

Fruit preserves, as needed

2 tbsp (16 g) confectioners' sugar, for dusting (optional)

TORTE NAPOLEON

Торт Наполеон ✤ Tort Napoleon

Torte Napoleon is a classic, iconic Russian cake recipe that never gets old. This French-inspired cake is very popular in Russia and throughout Eastern Europe—and every celebration must have one! The recipe does take some time to make, but it's well worth the effort for a special occasion. For best results, allow the cake to set in the refrigerator overnight.

YIELD: 12 TO 16 SERVINGS

To make the pastry, place the butter in a medium bowl and chill it in the freezer for 20 minutes. Place half the butter and 2¾ cups (344 g) of the flour in a food processor and pulse for 1 minute, until fine crumbs form. Transfer the flour and butter mixture to a large bowl. Repeat this process with the remaining butter and 2¾ cups (344 g) of flour.

In a large measuring cup or bowl, combine the eggs, water, vodka, vinegar and sea salt. Whisk the ingredients together for 1 minute. Create a well in the flour mixture and pour in the egg mixture. Use a spatula to combine the ingredients, creating a soft dough. Once the dough starts to come together, start mixing it with your hands.

Knead the dough minimally, just until the flour is incorporated and no dry patches remain. Using a sharp knife, divide the dough evenly into twelve pieces. Roll each piece gently into a ball, then place them on a medium baking sheet. Cover the baking sheet with plastic wrap and chill the dough for about 1 hour in the refrigerator or 30 minutes in the freezer.

After chilling the dough, preheat the oven to 400°F (204°C). Line two (12 x 17–inch [30 x 43–cm]) baking sheets with silicone mats or parchment paper. Work with one piece of dough at a time; keep the rest chilled. Use a rolling pin to roll out the dough into a 9-inch (23-cm) circle directly on the silicone mat or parchment paper. Using an 8-inch (20-cm) pan or round piece of paper as a guide, cut the dough to size. Keep the scraps on the baking sheets and save the baked scraps for garnishing the cake.

Bake the pastry for 10 minutes, until it is golden brown. Cool the layer on a wire rack and place the scraps in a plastic zip-top bag. Prepare the remaining layers the same way. Use alternate baking sheets for each layer, allowing the baking sheets to cool completely before using them again. To speed up the baking process, a larger baking sheet may be used to fit two layers per baking sheet. If the layers are shrinking too much during baking, allow the dough to chill for an additional 30 minutes.

(Continued)

PASTRY

1¾ cups (392 g) butter, cubed

5½ cups (688 g) all-purpose flour

2 large eggs

⅔ cup (160 ml) cold water

3 tbsp (45 ml) vodka

1 tbsp (15 ml) distilled white vinegar

¼ tsp fine sea salt

TORTE NAPOLEON (CONTINUED)

While the dough is chilling, prepare the custard. Place the egg yolks and sugar in a large bowl. In a small ramekin, combine the cornstarch and water and stir to create a slurry. Add the slurry to the egg yolks, then whisk vigorously for 2 to 3 minutes, until the mixture is light and creamy.

Combine the milk and flour in a large pot, whisking for 1 minute, until the mixture is smooth. Cook the milk mixture for 3 to 4 minutes over medium heat, stirring occasionally, until the milk is steaming but not boiling. Slowly add 1 cup (240 ml) of the milk mixture at a time to the egg yolk mixture, stirring well after each addition.

Once the two mixtures have been combined, pour the custard base into the pot. Cook the custard over medium-low heat, stirring constantly with a rubber spatula, for 8 to 10 minutes, until the custard thickens into a pudding. It should hold its shape on the back of a spoon. If the custard starts to clump, whisk for 1 minute, until it is smooth.

Once the custard has thickened, remove it from the heat and add the butter and vanilla. Whisk until the butter is completely melted. Cover the custard with a lid or plastic wrap and let it cool completely in the refrigerator.

Once the custard and pastry layers have cooled, assemble the cake. First, soak each pastry layer lightly with the tea using a pastry brush. Add approximately ¼ cup (60 g) of the custard between each layer, using an offset spatula to spread the custard evenly. Use the remaining custard to frost the top and sides of the cake.

To garnish the cake, crush the scrap pastry pieces into fine crumbs with a rolling pin. Gently press the crumbs into the sides and top of the cake. Allow the cake to set and chill in the refrigerator overnight. When you are ready to serve, remove the cake from the refrigerator at least 1 hour prior to allow the layers to soften.

To make the optional chocolate ganache, place the semisweet chocolate chips and cream in a medium measuring cup, then heat them in the microwave for 1 minute, or until the cream is hot. Allow the chocolate to stand for 1 minute, then stir the mixture until the chocolate is completely smooth. Gently spread the chocolate ganache onto the cake, then pipe circles of the white chocolate onto the ganache. Use a toothpick to create a spiderweb effect.

CUSTARD

6 large egg yolks

⅔ cup (132 g) granulated sugar

¼ cup (36 g) cornstarch

¼ cup (60 ml) water

3 cups (720 ml) whole milk

2 tbsp (16 g) all-purpose flour

1 cup (224 g) unsalted butter

2 tsp (10 ml) pure vanilla extract

Sweetened black tea, as needed

OPTIONAL CHOCOLATE GANACHE

½ cup (88 g) semisweet chocolate chips

¼ cup (60 ml) cream

¼ cup (44 g) white chocolate chips, melted

WARM FRUIT KISSEL

Кисель ❖ Kisel'

Fruit kissel is one of the most popular fruit desserts in Eastern Europe. This warm jelly is made with loads of berries and fruit and just a touch of sugar. Cornstarch is added as a thickening agent, creating an almost soup-like dish. Enjoy this recipe year-round with fresh fruit in the summer and frozen fruit in the winter. I like to make this recipe with a variety of fruits, such as peaches, strawberries, cherries, apples, pears and blueberries.

YIELD: 14 CUPS (4.5 KG)

6 cups (750 g) mixed fruit and berries

8¼ cups (2 L) water, divided

¾ cup (150 g) granulated sugar

¼ cup (36 g) cornstarch

Wash and clean the fruit, and slice any larger fruit (such as apples) into bite-size pieces. Place the fruit, 8 cups (1.9 L) of the water and sugar into a large pot over high heat. Bring the mixture to a boil, then reduce the heat to medium and cook the fruit for 8 to 9 minutes.

In a small bowl, combine the cornstarch with the remaining ¼ cup (60 ml) of water and stir until a smooth slurry forms. Pour the slurry into the pot and cook the kissel for 1 minute, until the mixture thickens.

Pour the hot kissel into smaller serving dishes or into a large punch bowl. Allow the kissel to stand for at least 30 to 60 minutes, until it has slightly cooled and thickened. Keep leftover kissel refrigerated and reheat it when you are ready to serve.

WARM FRUIT COMPOTE

Компот ❖ Compot

In Ukraine and Russia, the choice drink for every day and most occasions is compote. This sweet and flavorful fruit drink is made by boiling together various fruits and berries, along with a touch of sugar. It can be enjoyed warm in the winter months and chilled in the summer. It's also great as a mixer—just add 1 shot (30 ml) of vodka per 1 cup (240 ml) of compote.

12 cups (2.9 L) water

½ to 1 cup (100 to 200 g) granulated sugar

6 to 7 cups (750 g) fresh or frozen fruit and/or berries

YIELD: ABOUT 16 CUPS (3.8 L)

In a large pot, combine the water, sugar and fruit and/or berries.

Bring the compote to a boil over high heat and cook for 10 to 15 minutes (boil for a shorter time if you are using soft fruit). Turn the heat off and allow the compote to stand at room temperature and cool completely.

After the compote has cooled completely, pour it into a glass pitcher or punch bowl. Keep the compote refrigerated. The compote will stand in the fridge for 1 week. Serve it chilled or warm.

QUICK TIP: If you need inspiration, try some of these flavor variations:

- Apricot, peach or nectarine, strawberry, raspberry

- Sweet cherries, tart pie cherries, raspberry

- Blackberry, raspberry, blueberry, strawberry

- Apple, pear, cranberry, raspberry

APPLE KVASS

Яблочный Квас ✦ Yabluchniy Kvass

Kvass is a traditional Eastern European fermented beverage made with yeast or bread and sometimes fruit, like this apple version. There are also honey, beet, barley, berry and even mint varieties! Kvass is truly an old-world drink, with roots that can be traced back millennia and with early mentions found in writings dating back to the 900s. It's a refreshing, effervescent beverage that's great on hot summer days. The fermentation process takes a few days and shouldn't be rushed. If available, use dark rye bread for a more traditional flavor.

YIELD: 10 CUPS (2.4 L)

7 large apples (any variety), divided

16 cups (3.8 L) water

1 to 1½ cups (200 to 300 g) granulated sugar

2 tsp (6 g) active dry yeast

½ cup (60 g) dried cranberries

1 (6-inch [15-cm]) long piece French baguette or rye bread

2 (3-inch [8-cm]) cinnamon sticks (optional)

Leave the apples unpeeled and cut six of them into quarters. Place the quartered apples and water into a large pot over high heat. Bring the apples to a boil, reduce the heat to medium and simmer for 10 minutes, stirring occasionally. Remove the pot from the heat and allow the juice and apples to cool to room temperature.

Once they have cooled, transfer the apples and juice to a large glass container or glass drink dispenser jar. Add the sugar, yeast and cranberries and stir until the sugar is dissolved. Break the bread apart into 1-inch (2.5-cm) pieces and add them to the mixture. Add the cinnamon sticks, if using. Grate the remaining apple and add it to the jar. Stir everything together for 1 minute, until the ingredients are well combined.

Cover the glass jar or dispenser with a cheesecloth and hold the cheesecloth in place with a rubber band. Place the jar in a dark area, away from sunlight. Allow the apples and bread to ferment for 2 to 3 days. Once the fermentation starts, it will be visible: A fluffy white foam will start to form on the top of the apples and bread.

Once the fermentation is visible and strong, drain the kvass. Line a fine-mesh strainer with cheesecloth and strain the juice twice, discarding everything else. Wash the glass jar or dispenser and pour the kvass back into it for storage. Once done, the kvass needs to be refrigerated and is best served very cold.

KOROLEVSKI TORTE

Королевский Торт ✣ Korolevskiy Tort

"Korolevski torte" literally translates to "king's cake," and this stunning cake really is worthy of royalty. This old-world Russian cake was traditionally made in the imperial cities of Russia and enjoyed by the aristocracy. It's made with three different sour cream cake layers: chocolate, pecan and poppy seed–cranberry. Sour cream is used very often in Eastern European baking, and here it makes the cake layers very soft and moist. Garnish the cake with chocolate ganache and chocolate lace for a truly impressive king's cake!

YIELD: 12 TO 16 SERVINGS

To make the cake, preheat the oven to 350°F (177°C). Prepare three (8-inch [20-cm]) cake pans by lining the bottoms with parchment paper and spraying the sides with nonstick spray.

In a large bowl, combine the eggs, sour cream, sugar and vanilla. Whisk for 3 to 4 minutes, until the mixture is smooth. In a separate large bowl, combine the flour and baking powder. Sift the flour into the egg mixture, then whisk for 1 minute, just until the flour is incorporated.

Divide the cake batter evenly between three medium bowls. To the first bowl, add the melted chocolate chips and whisk for about 1 minute, until the chocolate is mixed into the batter. To the second bowl, add the pecans and stir the nuts into the batter. To the third bowl, add the poppy seeds and dried cranberries and stir until they are mixed into the batter.

Pour the cake batters into the prepared pans. Bake them for 26 to 28 minutes. The top of the cake layers will have a slightly bumpy texture and they will not rise too much. Remove the layers from the oven and let them cool completely on a wire rack. Once the layers have cooled completely, use a sharp serrated knife to split the layers in half horizontally, creating six layers total.

(Continued)

CAKE

6 large eggs

3 cups (720 g) sour cream

2 cups (400 g) granulated sugar

2 tsp (10 ml) pure vanilla extract

3 cups (375 g) all-purpose flour

1 tbsp (12 g) baking powder

1 cup (175 g) dark chocolate chips, melted

1 cup (125 g) diced pecans

¼ cup (31 g) poppy seeds

½ cup (60 g) dried cranberries

1 cup (240 ml) sweetened black tea

KOROLEVSKI TORTE (CONTINUED)

While the cake layers are cooling, prepare the frosting. Place the butter in the bowl of a stand mixer and whisk on high speed for 5 to 6 minutes, until the butter is white and fluffy, scraping down the sides of the bowl often. (Alternatively, you may prepare the frosting in a large bowl using a handheld mixer.) Add the vanilla, salt and dulce de leche and whisk again for 1 minute. Add the confectioners' sugar. Whisk the frosting for 3 to 4 minutes, scraping down the sides of the bowl to incorporate everything.

Assemble the cake with alternating cake layers: chocolate layer, pecan layer, poppy seed–cranberry layer and then repeat the arrangement again. When placing each layer, lightly soak it with the tea using a pastry brush. Spread a generous amount of frosting between each cake layer, then frost the top and sides. Smooth the frosting using an offset spatula. If desired, transfer some frosting to a pastry bag for garnishing the cake later (I use an open French star tip). Transfer the cake to the refrigerator to chill for 30 minutes prior to adding the chocolate ganache.

To make the chocolate ganache, heat the cream in a small bowl in the microwave or in a small pot on the stove until it is hot. Place the chocolate chips in a medium bowl and pour the hot milk over them. Allow the chocolate to stand for 2 to 3 minutes, then whisk the ganache until it's smooth. Allow the ganache to cool until just slightly warm to the touch. Pour it along the edges of the cake first, and then fill in the center. Decorate the cake with dollops of frosting and garnish it with the pecan halves, if using.

To make white chocolate lace, melt the white chocolate melts, then transfer the white chocolate to a zip-top bag and cut off a tiny bit of one corner to create a pastry bag. Lay out squares of parchment paper and drizzle the white chocolate on them, forming small "lace" pieces. To create curved pieces, place the squares into a glass and allow the white chocolate to set.

FROSTING

2 cups (448 g) unsalted butter, softened

1 tsp pure vanilla extract

¼ tsp salt

1 (14-oz [392-g]) can dulce de leche

2 cups (250 g) confectioners' sugar

CHOCOLATE GANACHE

¼ cup (60 ml) cream

½ cup (88 g) semisweet chocolate chips

GARNISHES

Pecan halves (optional)

½ cup (88 g) white chocolate melts

ACKNOWLEDGMENTS

This book wouldn't be possible without the strong, persevering spirit of the Eastern European people, people who are devoted to sticking to their traditions and passing them on. Thank you to all my Ukrainian, Russian, Polish and Romanian family and extended family for keeping the traditions going through every imaginable event.

A huge thank-you to my parents, who left everything behind in the USSR to come to the United States and give our family a better life. Thank you for instilling in me a love for Eastern European cuisine. I would not be where I am today without your dedication.

A special thank-you to my wonderful and talented sister, Nina. Thank you so much for all your help with this book, for being my right-hand lady, washing my dishes, grocery shopping and prepping my ingredients when I couldn't. I couldn't have written this one without you.

Thank you to my editor, Sarah, and my publisher, William, as well as the entire team at Page Street Publishing for believing in me and giving me the incredible opportunity to author a second cookbook. I hope you enjoy these recipes for years to come.

Thank you to my amazing husband for always being supportive of my food career from day one. You're the best food critic and partner anyone could ask for.

ABOUT THE AUTHOR

Tatyana Nesteruk is a food blogger, YouTube video creator and cookbook author of *The European Cake Cookbook*. Her recipes and videos can be found on her blog, Tatyana's Everyday Food. Tatyana has appeared on the *Today* show several times and many local TV channels, sharing her Eastern European recipes. She partners frequently with household names such as Smithfield, Pompeian, Holland House and Barilla.

Tatyana was born in Yekaterinburg, Russia, and raised in Washington State in a tight-knit Slavic community. She learned to cook from her mother and grandmother, who passed down many of the recipes in this cookbook. Tatyana and her husband, Anatoliy, reside in California. In her spare time, she enjoys traveling, tennis, photography and studying science and medicine.

INDEX